Complaint
Management
Excelle nce

Complaint Management Excellence

Creating customer loyalty through service recovery

Sarah Cook

KoganPage

LONDON PHILADELPHIA NEW DELHI

First published in Great Britain and the United States in 2012 by Kogan Page Limited

120 Pentonville Road
London N1 9JN
United Kingdom
www.koganpage.com

1518 Walnut Street, Suite 1100
Philadelphia PA 19102
USA

4737/23 Ansari Road
Daryaganj
New Delhi 110002
India

© Sarah Cook, 2012

The right of Sarah Cook to be identified as the author of this work has been asserted by her in accordance with the Copyright, Designs and Patents Act 1988.

ISBN   978 0 7494 6530 8
E-ISBN   978 0 7494 6531 5

British Library Cataloguing-in-Publication Data

A CIP record for this book is available from the British Library.

Library of Congress Cataloging-in-Publication Data

Cook, Sarah.
    Complaint management excellence : creating customer loyalty through service recovery / Sarah Cook.
      p. cm.
    ISBN 978-0-7494-6530-8 – ISBN 978-0-7494-6531-5 (ebook)   1. Consumer complaints.
2. Customer loyalty. 3. Customer services. I. Title.
    HF5415.52.C66 2012
    658.8'12–dc23

                                                                                        2011045182

Typeset by Graphicraft Limited, Hong Kong
Printed and bound in India by Replika Press Pvt Ltd

CONTENTS

LIST OF FIGURES
AND TABLES

Figures

Table

PREFACE

In the global economy customers' expectations are continually rising. However, many businesses fail to deliver against expectations. Whereas in the past customers have not always been forthcoming in expressing their dissatisfaction, today they are more vocal and informed of their rights. The growth of social media has also played a part in shaping customers' views and opinions. Companies that do not manage customer dissatisfaction well, risk not only losing existing customers but alienating potential ones.

Yet research shows that when companies deal with complaints well they actively encourage loyalty. In fact a customer who has complained and whose complaint is dealt with well is more likely to be an advocate of a business than a customer who has not complained at all.

My aim in *Complaint Management Excellence* is to provide practical advice, tools and techniques for managers to effectively manage complaints in their organization. Rather than seeing complaining customers as a nuisance, best practice is to view complaints as an opportunity to put things right, not just for the complainant but also for other customers. This improves the long-term prospects of the company, not only by increasing customer service levels and enhancing products and services but also by improving employee morale and engagement.

The reality is that even the best of companies sometimes get things wrong. In order to arrive at a culture where complaints are welcomed, the underlying values, processes, structure, strategy and people in an organization need to be aligned to customer needs.

This book provides practical examples, case studies and research from across the globe about how to manage complaints effectively and engender an organizational culture that is customer focused. I hope that you find the book insightful and useful.

Sarah Cook
The Stairway Consultancy Ltd
sarah@thestairway.co.uk
www.thestairway.co.uk

ABOUT THE AUTHOR

Sarah Cook is the Managing Director of The Stairway Consultancy Ltd. She has 20 years' consulting experience specializing in customer service and culture change. Prior to this Sarah worked for Unilever and as Head of Customer Care for a retail consultancy.

Sarah has wide experience of helping public and private sector organizations improve their complaint management and customer service. She works in the UK and on a global basis.

Sarah regularly speaks at conferences on customer service, complaint management and culture change. She is a business author with 35 books and manuals published. Other titles published by Kogan Page include:

- *Customer Care Excellence;*
- *Practical Guide to Employee Engagement;*
- *Change Management Excellence.*

Sarah has an MA in modern languages from Cambridge University, and gained an MBA in 1991. She is a Fellow of the Chartered Institute of Personnel Development and a Chartered Marketer. Sarah is a judge at the National Customer Service Awards. She is passionate about excellent service.

Complaints as opportunities

Welcome to *Complaint Management Excellence*.

In this first chapter I set out:

- the social, technological, political and economic factors that are changing customer expectations of the service they experience;
- how this is impacting on customer satisfaction and the complaints customers make to organizations;
- why complaints are important to organizations, and the risks associated with handling complaints badly;
- why best-practice organizations view complaints as an opportunity for improvement.

The chapter ends with some questions to help you assess how well your organization views complaints as an opportunity to improve the products and services it provides to customers.

Increasing customer expectations

The number of complaints is on the rise across the globe as customers are no longer prepared to put up with poor service. Undoubtedly businesses in the 21st century are now more focused on the need to deliver an excellent customer experience, yet many do not welcome complaints or encourage their employees to see them as opportunities for improvement. They view complaints as an unnecessary evil rather than an incentive to learn and improve as a business.

I certainly could not begin talking about complaints without focusing on customers and the trends that impact on their expectations of the service they receive.

Today's customer is far more informed and vocal than when I first started in the customer-service industry over 20 years ago. Then, customer service as a profession was in its infancy. Power lay with large manufacturing companies who dominated the marketplace and who were chiefly concerned with satisfying their distributors. The focus was on business to business (B2B) rather than business to the consumer.

In the intervening years, the way we live and our expectations as customers have changed dramatically. Today is a much faster-moving society where customers are better informed, more knowledgeable and better travelled. Globalization has led to greater choice for customers. As marketplaces have become more sophisticated, there has been a growth in service industries rather than in manufacturing in many parts of the world. For example, according to the Office for National Statistics, in the UK manufacturing industry accounted for 40 per cent of jobs in post-war Britain, compared with 8 per cent today.

In Western society, increasing economic pressures mean that today's consumers seek excellent service as well as value for money. In emerging markets such as Brazil and India there is a growing middle class who are attracted to brands that offer good-quality service. In countries such as China and Russia, there is strong demand for luxury consumer goods and the levels of service that are expected of these. As a consequence, many more organizations are aware of the need to deliver an outstanding customer experience.

Service organizations such as retailer Nordstrom and low-cost carrier Southwest Airlines, both based in the United States, were at the vanguard of a sea-change in how organizations viewed their customers. These companies developed a culture of customer excellence that transformed the way businesses thought and interacted with their customers. Management gurus, starting with Tom Peters, encouraged a generation of business leaders to aim to differentiate their companies from their competitors via the quality of service they provided. Professors Heskett, Sasser and Schlesinger's book *The Service Profit Chain*, published in 1997, established the link between high levels of employee satisfaction and engagement and great customer service.

Today, countries such as Singapore, the UK, the Netherlands, the United States and Canada have sophisticated customer-service industries that operate in mature marketplaces. Customer service in these countries is typically aimed at retaining customers and preventing churn. In the UK for example, customer contact centres are now the norm when dealing with customers in the banking, telecommunications, retail, IT and insurance industries. Contact centres employ approximately 4 per cent of the UK workforce.

Customer service in countries such as Turkey, South Africa and Russia is focused on building relationships with customers, whereas in emerging markets such as Brazil, Peru, China and India customer service is aimed at acquiring new customers.

The power of the customer

Not only has the structure of business changed, but in recent years customers have become more empowered. No longer prepared to accept poor service, power now increasingly lies with the consumer.

There are a number of reasons for this, some of which I have touched on above:

- Today we live in a fast-moving society where people are time and attention poor.
- There is more competition in the marketplace and therefore more consumer choice.
- De-regulation and in some cases government regulation have opened up marketplaces to more competition and greater customer empowerment.
- The economic climate, particularly in the Western hemisphere, has led to a greater emphasis on cost and value for money, driving down prices and increasing the need for high-quality service in order to differentiate.
- People are more travelled and better informed.

- There is increasing demand for international brands and corresponding service experience.

In addition, one of the biggest influencers is the rapid growth of social media.

Social media

'Word of click' is now becoming more powerful than 'word of mouth'. Increasingly people throughout the globe are using the internet, and the voice of the consumer has more power than that of today's organizations. In March 2011 Internet World Stats claimed that 31 per cent of the world's population use the internet. This figure varies from 78 per cent penetration in North America to 11 per cent in Africa. In the year 2010–11, there was a 480 per cent increase overall in its use. The internet has been adopted worldwide faster than any other modern invention such as the telephone or television. Sites such as Facebook, Twitter and LinkedIn have grown in popularity and have been instrumental in social change.

But it is not laptops, tablets and PCs that are being used most to access the internet; research by mobiThinking.com shows that half a billion people accessed the internet using mobile phones in 2010. Seventy-seven per cent of the world's population owned mobile phones in 2010 and there were 5.3 billion subscribers. The Japanese are the world's most sophisticated mobile users while China has the fastest growing usage.

By 2016 application-to-person messaging (A2P) is expected to overtake person-to-person SMS. This will include offers from retailers and updates from banks as well as m-payments. It is estimated that between 500 million and 1 billion people will access financial services by mobile phone (tap-and-go) in the next five years to make payments and transfers. In China alone, it is estimated there will be 169 million users of tap-and-go payments in 2013. M-ticketing for airline, rail and bus travel, festivals, cinemas and sports events will become the norm.

Generation Ys, the people born between 1977 and 1994 as well as Generation Zs (those born after 1995) have an inseparable connection to technology, and this is spilling over into older generations. New communication channels are altering customers' expectations about service. Internet-based social networking is giving customers a vehicle for spreading good and bad news at the click of a mouse. The effect of the rise in access to social media is that the customers of today and the future are more likely to trust their peers than the organizations from which they buy products and services. Aggregator sites such as TripAdvisor, Amazon and eBay, which constantly provide customer feedback, are examples of how customers can shape future purchasing choices. Jeff Bezoz of Amazon.com is quoted as saying: 'If you make customers unhappy in the physical world, they might each tell six friends. If you make customers unhappy on the internet, they can each tell 6,000 friends.'

Delivering excellent service

One organization that has taken account of trends in customer service to deliver beyond expectations is Zappos. Zappos is an online shoe retailer in the United States that has won outstanding acclaim from its customers for the level of service it provides. It is also ranked in the top three most admired companies for its customer experience by customer-service professionals (along with Apple and Amazon). Founded in 1999, within 10 years it had a turnover of $1bn and was ranked by *Fortune* magazine as 23rd on its list of the best companies to work for.

From its foundation Zappos aimed to deliver 'wow' through service. Customer service is a core element of its culture, and it hires employees who are passionate about service. Zappos offers customers over 90,000 styles of shoes online in every size and in more than 500 brands. It only lists product on its site that it holds in stock. It has a 365-day return policy so customers can try on shoes in their own home and return them within a year at no charge if they are not suitable. It offers free shipping and returns and 24/7 availability. Zappos invested in its own distribution centre which stays open round the clock so that someone can order at 11 pm at night and still receive their shoes the next day.

Agents in Zappos' call centre are encouraged to be themselves and to build great relationships with customers. They have no scripts or restrictions to how long they are on a call to a customer. They also answer e-mails from customers and monitor Twitter and other social networking sites so that they can respond quickly to customers' queries and concerns. There is a resource-desk team who answer more complex questions about the shoes that customers request, such as heel height, fit and colour. Employees are empowered to take action to make customers happy. For example, they can send flowers or offer repeat customers upgrades to free overnight or second-day delivery. They can use their own discretion to put things right for customers and retain their loyalty if things go wrong and there are complaints.

Zappos recruits new employees on the basis of their ability to do the job and their cultural fit. It has an extensive induction programme for all employees that includes everyone spending four weeks in its contact centre and one week in its warehouse facility. During induction new recruits focus on the corporate culture and behaviours needed to deliver excellent service. Zappos is transparent with its employees, customers and suppliers. The company's extranet, for example, lets vendors see which shoes are selling and how profitably.

Rather than spending on advertising, Zappos has relied on word of mouth and social media to help grow the business, confident that the excellent service it provides will generate promoters for the brand. Zappos was sold to Amazon in 2009 but still operates as a successful independent entity.

Levels of customer satisfaction

Zappos is an example of a company with a reputation for excellent customer service. However, there are many organizations that do not satisfy their customers and these customers are far more likely to express their negative emotions and to tell other people too.

Figure 1.1 illustrates the potential stages that customers go through in their relationship with organizations. At the base level, customers receive sub-standard service that does not meet their expectations. The customers have three choices at this level about how to act: to complain to the organization, to voice their dissatisfaction to others, or to say or do nothing. Potentially they can remain a customer of the organization, or decide to leave.

If the service customers receive is satisfactory and meets their expectations, they still make a choice: whether to stay with the organization or to look elsewhere for a similar product or service. At this level the customer's relationship with the organization is transactional and the customer is likely to deal with the organization on a rational level.

FIGURE 1.1 The customer-advocacy pyramid

Level 3 of the pyramid is when the customers become emotionally engaged. They receive service above and beyond their expectations and they in turn are delighted. At this stage their loyalty to the organization increases. (If a complaint is handled well, a business can also ensure that their customers reach this level of delight. I will discuss this in more detail later.)

Level 4, the pinnacle of the pyramid, is when customers have consistently been delighted with the service they have received. They love the organization that is providing the service and actively promote it to their friends and acquaintances. These customers are called 'promoters', a term first used in 2003 by Fred Reichheld from the consultancy Bain & Company in an article called 'The one number you need to grow'.

Promoters are customers who rate the answer to the question 'How likely is it that you would recommend our company to a friend or a colleague?' on a 0–10 rating scale as 9 or 10. Reichheld, Bain & Company and Satmetrix developed the customer loyalty measure called the Net Promoter Score (NPS). NPS is a number either above or below zero. The higher the positive Net Promoter Score, the greater the number of loyal customers your business has. This is arrived at by taking the number of promoters (customers who score 9 or 10 out of 10) from the number of detractors (customers who score 0 to 6 out of 10).

An NPS can be as low as −100 (everybody is a detractor) or as high as +100 (everybody is a promoter). A company with an NPS of 50 or more is considered to be excellent. The Net Promoter company Satmetrix publishes a Net Promoter Industry Benchmark. In 2011 companies with the highest NPSs in their sector included well-known brands such as USAA, JetBlue Airways, Symantec, Trader Joe's, Vanguard, Amazon.com, Apple, Google, Costco and American Express.

Customer complaints

Unfortunately, many companies have negative NPSs. This indicates that there are many customers who receive a level of service that is below their expectations and become detractors of the organization. At this point the customer may decide to complain.

Research in the UK by the Institute of Customer Service reveals that around three-quarters of customers are prepared to complain, compared with about half some 10 years ago. Think of a poor example of customer service that you have received recently and I am sure that something will come to mind. Psychologists believe that negative experiences are more memorable than positive ones. In developing the contents for this book, I asked various colleagues, friends and clients for examples of when they have been dissatisfied about the service they received and what they did about it. Here is an example that I received in an e-mail of the kind of things that make customers dissatisfied:

> Yesterday I was waiting in for an engineer to come to activate my phone line. The highlights of the engineer's visit were:
>
> ● He asked me how much I paid to rent my flat and advised me that renting was a bad idea and that everyone should be on the property ladder like him. When I explained I had no deposit for a house, he advised me to gamble everything I have on Arsenal and Manchester United winning each week; over the course of a season I was bound to have enough money!
>
> ● He explained that his current employer was rubbish and that he previously worked for another telephone provider for 10 years and they were very good. I asked him why he didn't work for them anymore. His answer was, because he was sacked.
>
> ● He had a couple of colleagues come around and assist him. It was all looking good, but after they left the engineer couldn't get the phone line to work. He suggested to me that his colleagues had sabotaged his work so somebody else would get the credit of finishing the job instead of him.

- He twice went to check the 'cab'. It turns out this is a box down the street where all the phone lines go into. Both times he was gone for over an hour. I do suspect he may have been in the pub across the road from the cab.

- Whilst in my presence he took a call from a colleague and explained to him how his manager 'did a disciplinary' with him that morning and had accused him of gross misconduct. Apparently he swore at his manager and didn't answer his phone. He then decided to fill me in with all the details: he openly told me that he may have an attitude problem and that is why he may have got into trouble.

- He seemed to be talking to himself on numerous occasions and swearing at himself.

- He told me that he was going to take the following week off work to consult legal advice about his disciplinary.

- All in all from start to finish he was on the job for nearly five hours and seemingly achieved nothing; he advised me another engineer would contact me.

- He rang me today to enquire whether he had left some tools at my flat.*

* Thanks to Callum Lafferty of Waitrose who was the customer in this example.

Unfortunately I am sure that many other people have had similar experiences as customers. The issue today is that consumers are no longer prepared to put up with poor service. If we do not complain directly to the organization, we certainly do tell other people. Businesses are as much at the mercy of the 'power of the internet' and social networking as they are negative word of mouth.

What is a complaint?

The best definition I believe of a complaint is 'any expression of dissatisfaction'. It does not matter whether the complaint comes from an existing customer or not, or whether the complaint is justified or not. If someone is unhappy with a service or product and voices their concern, this counts as a complaint and should be taken seriously.

There is an international standards programme for complaints, called ISO 10002:2004. Its definition is: 'A complaint is an expression of dissatisfaction made to an organization related to its products, or the complaint-handling process itself, where a response or resolution is explicitly or implicitly expected.'

Customer dissatisfaction

There are numerous studies around customer complaints. The overriding findings show that only the minority of customers who are dissatisfied do in fact complain. This is often likened to an iceberg: the tip of the iceberg represents those customers who directly voice their concerns to the organization (Figure 1.2). Underneath the waterline are the vast majority of customers who do not complain.

FIGURE 1.2 The complaints iceberg

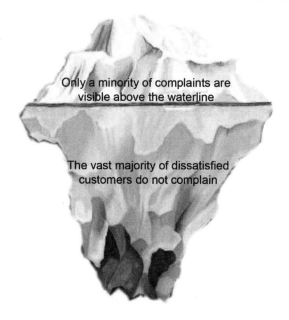

Only a minority of complaints are visible above the waterline

The vast majority of dissatisfied customers do not complain

For example, overall it is estimated that one in four people is unhappy with the products and services received, yet overall only one in 26 bothers to complain directly to the organization. The other 96 per cent either feel complaining is not worth the effort, or do not know how to complain or who to contact. Of the 4 per cent who complain, only about 50 per cent report a satisfactory problem resolution.

Other statistics demonstrate the need for organizations to actively welcome complaints and to make it easy for customers to complain.

It is estimated that:

- Of the three out of four customers who are dissatisfied and do not complain directly to the organization, at least half just stop buying or dealing with the organization if they have an alternative. In one financial services organization that we deal with, for example, studies show that customers who complain and whose complaint is not dealt with well are twice as likely not to take up other products and services from the company, and three times as likely to close their account.

- The average company loses 10 per cent of its customers each year. On average a dissatisfied customer tells at least 10 other people about any poor experience, whereas they only tell three people if they have a good experience as a customer. The 10 people who have heard about the poor experience from the customer will tell at least five other people.

- On the internet, this figure is considerably more.

The above figures do not take into account the use of social media; the anonymity it allows is leading to more dissatisfaction being voiced online. Research from Euro RSCG Worldwide shows that nearly 43 per cent of US internet users feel less inhibited online, with the effect most prominent among females and users aged 25 to 54.

In the research, customers reported they were also more likely to 'lash out' on the web when they had something to say about a company or brand. A fifth of internet users, including almost a quarter of men, had done so. The more interactions happen online with no direct contact with a company, the more likely they are to tilt toward extreme behaviour.

One example of the negative publicity that can be generated via social media is what happened to the cable network company Comcast in the United States when one customer had a poor customer experience. The customer had made numerous calls to the organization in order to resolve a problem with its cable network, and had waited in for a service engineer to call but had numerous missed appointments. When the service engineer did eventually arrive, the customer left him to complete the work. The service engineer fell asleep on the customer's couch while waiting on hold on the telephone to the local Comcast office. The customer's teenage son used the camera on his mobile phone to shoot a video of the engineer. The customer was so upset by this experience that he decided to post the video clip on YouTube. To date there have been 1.6 million viewings of it.

As a result of the harmful publicity this generated, Comcast created the position of Digital Detective. It has team members scanning the internet and social networking sites looking for comments customers make about their company and offering help and support in relation to issues and complaints.

Regulatory bodies are now also taking a greater interest in the number of complaints that consumers make. There is a trend towards publishing complaints league tables that list all the companies in a sector and how many complaints they receive. In the UK for example, the communications regulator Ofcom publishes quarterly complaint-handling data about major telecoms providers. This aims to provide useful information for consumers and also to push telecoms providers towards improving their performance.

Here is the complaints iceberg illustrating the negative power of complaints using the figures above. This is based on TARP research conducted in 1999 but with the addition of social media, I am sure still holds true today; particularly when you consider the power of the internet.

FIGURE 1.3 The negative power of complaints

1
unhappy customer
complains to an organisation

24 unhappy customers do not complain

They tell on average 10 other people

Those people tell at least
5 other people

At least 1,200 people therefore
hear about poor service

The risks involved in poor complaint handling

So there are numerous potential risks to an organization if complaints are not handled well. From a customer's perspective there is the irritation and frustration experienced by the minority of people who do try to complain directly to the organization but find it difficult to know where to complain, or who are met by indifference and lack of care about their needs. For the organization the customer risk in ineffective complaint resolution results in:

- reduced customer trust and loyalty;
- reduced uptake of products and services;
- customer attrition;
- customers becoming detractors, actively criticizing the organization and not recommending it to others.

Ineffective use of complaints information can result in continued customer dissatisfaction with recurring issues. Poor complaint handling is estimated to result in between 5 and 15 per cent lower revenues, and corresponding reductions in profits. When an organization does not welcome complaints, this can result in a huge hidden cost as a business does not have any feedback from customers about why they are defecting.

As we have seen, there is also a reputational risk for the organization when complaints are not dealt with fairly, resulting in criticism not only by customers but by non-governmental organizations, media, consumer associations and trade organizations.

In addition, as many companies operate in a regulatory environment, there is a risk of non-compliance with relevant regulation and legislation, resulting in regulatory censure, sanctions, fines, withdrawal of licence to operate, and capital and revenue loss. For example, in July 2011 in the UK, energy provider British Gas was fined £2.5 million by the energy regulator Ofgem for the mishandling of customer complaints.

British Gas is the UK's largest energy supplier, serving nearly half of British households. Specifically, Ofgem found that British Gas failed to re-open complaints when customers indicated that their complaint was not resolved, and that the company did not have adequate procedures in place for dealing with complaints from micro businesses employing fewer than 10 people. This was the largest fine that Ofgem has made to date in terms of customer service and was indicative of its, and other regulators', aim to ensure suppliers treat customers fairly and transparently.

In the financial services sector in the UK, ineffective complaint resolution and use of complaints information can result in regulator intervention and enforcement action. Banks and insurance companies also run the risk of incurring costs in relation to independent arbitration services, such as the Financial Ombudsman Service fees in the UK.

There are also risks to a business operationally if complaints are not welcomed and dealt with well. Staff morale can be affected if they are not given appropriate training in how to deal with complaints, and when they see recurring complaints not being addressed. In addition staff capacity can be wasted in recording repeat complaint details.

If businesses do not seek to learn from complaints and make effective use of complaints information, they will not be able to address the root causes of problems. Therefore they will lack the ability to improve their products, services, processes and policies. In addition they will not be able to identify and address ineffective complaint-handling procedures or complaint handlers.

If businesses do not undertake root-cause analysis of why people are complaining, they will not see a reduction in complaints and therefore will continue to incur large handling costs. They may see a high volume of re-opened complaints that results in higher costs, including redress payments and loss of competitive advantage.

The positive power of effective complaint handling

The previous section dealt with the negative impact of not welcoming complaints and of not dealing with them fairly and effectively. However, we must not forget the positive power of complaints.

Studies show that, depending on the industry, 54–70 per cent of customers who register a complaint will do business with the organization again if their complaint is resolved in a timely and thoughtful fashion. The figure goes up to a staggering 95 per cent if the customer feels that the complaint was resolved quickly and fairly. In fact a well-handled complaint tends to breed more customer loyalty than the organization had before the negative incident. Typically customers whose complaints have been handled well rate their overall satisfaction and propensity to recommend the organization as 4 per cent higher than those who did not have a problem at all. In addition the customer is more likely to stay with the organization for longer, and some even spend more money than before.

Referring to the customer pyramid I mentioned earlier, a complaint is a 'moment of truth' and the way the organization deals with it either makes or breaks the emotional connection that the customer has with the business. When a complaint is handled well, the customer is more likely to become emotionally engaged with the organization and have a stronger desire to stay with the service provider. A customer can be transported from Level 1 to Level 3 on the pyramid.

FIGURE 1.4 The power of effective complaint handling

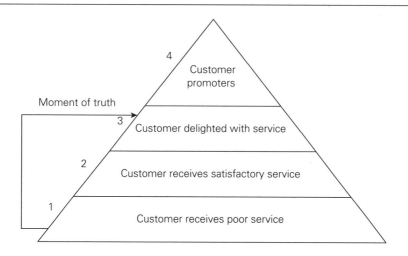

Furthermore, complaints can drive business improvement, improve internal communications and increase operational efficiency. In Australia for example, the Public Transportation Ombudsman made a study of the taxi and hire car industry in the state of Victoria; it found that when complaints were viewed positively and handled professionally and non-defensively, they drove industry improvement. This in turn led to fewer dissatisfied customers, increased customer loyalty and promoted greater confidence in the industry.

Complaints handled well can enhance a brand's reputation. A complaining customer who experiences a good recovery from a problem will become a promoter of the organization and build positive word of mouth (and clicks), openly spreading positive stories about their experience. Studies show that a 5 per cent reduction in the customer defection rate can increase profits by 25–85 per cent, depending on the industry. (All facts drawn from US Technical Assistance Research Program (TARP) Studies 1979–2010.)

A survey by American Express in the UK showed that more than half of customers would spend more on goods and services if the service experience was guaranteed to be first class.

One organization I am a big advocate of in the UK, and one that consistently tops the Institute of Customer Service league table for customer service, is retailer John Lewis and its supermarket arm, Waitrose. In surveys by retail analysts Verdict, John Lewis has been voted Britain's favourite retailer for four years running. Waitrose has also featured in the top 10 for many years and John Lewis online was voted best online retailer in 2010.

A personal example of how John Lewis deals with complaints is when I recently ordered a patio table and chairs for my deck. My husband and I went into a store and viewed their garden furniture range. On returning home I checked the measurements of the table and chairs and then placed an order online. I was delighted that the furniture turned up the next day and I duly placed the table and chairs on my deck. However, the first time we used the set, which happened to be at a barbecue with friends, I found the rubber stoppers on some of the legs were missing. This meant sitting on the chairs was rather perilous and we could not use them safely, so we and all our guests ended standing up. The following day I called John Lewis to complain. The lady I dealt with appeared genuinely sorry and offered to arrange for the rubber stoppers to be delivered to me so that the chairs could be made safe. A delivery van with the stoppers turned up the same day and the driver repaired the chairs and checked that these were then stable and safe on the deck. In the post the following day I received a John Lewis token for the inconvenience. The lady I had spoken with also called the day after to check that everything was now resolved to my satisfaction. For me this is an example of excellent complaint handling.

John Lewis's employees are all partners in the business and have a vested interest in the organization's success. Partners receive ongoing training on products, sales and service. They have expert product knowledge and go out of their way to deliver excellent service. To be able to do this consistently, John Lewis is keen to find opportunities to listen to customers, be open to feedback and act quickly on what customers tell them, particularly if they've got something wrong. The company uses customer surveys, panels, focus groups, online feedback forms and regular mystery shopping to help monitor levels of customer satisfaction and obtain a broad spectrum of customer opinion to respond to. For example, customers' views have driven the development of Waitrose's By Invitation and WaitroseDeliver services, as well as Quick Check, the scan-as-you-shop service. John Lewis aims to provide the best value on the high street by offering a 'Never Knowingly Undersold' promise to its customers, which is supported by excellent service.

Coincidentally, at the time of our visit to the store my husband misplaced his glasses – he thought that he had left them either at John Lewis or in one of the other two stores we visited that day. He phoned John Lewis and the other stores. John Lewis said that they would check their lost property and call back the next day, which they duly did. Neither of the other two stores returned the call. John Lewis called the next day and the day after to say they were sorry the glasses had not been handed in. Then on day four, they called again to say that my husband's glasses had been found in the furniture department. My husband was delighted and went to collect them. The assistant in the furniture department had these waiting for him and even gave his glasses a polish before she handed them back to him!

So, in summary, dealing with complaints well saves time and energy from both a customer and an employee perspective. Positive complaint handling saves time, money and materials, and highlights recurring quality or service delivery errors that can be fixed once and for all. It can also identify emerging issues and trends that the organization can address to gain better customer advocacy.

The business case for excellent complaint handling

I and my team of consultants are called in on assignments to help organizations be more customer focused where the business sees complaint handling as an unnecessary evil. In fact, my belief is that the way an organization handles complaints is an indicator of the quality of the customer experience it provides. Too many organizations attempt to minimize complaints and to save money by offering the minimum redress even when the complaint is justified.

Rather than seeing complaint handling as an unnecessary cost to the business, best-practice organizations view complaints as an investment in the organization's future. They actively welcome them and make it easy for customers to complain via whatever channel they choose. In addition they make complaints the lifeblood of their service and product improvements, using customer feedback to drive the continuous development of their business to better meet customer needs.

At telecoms company, Nokia, special agents are specifically trained in complaint-handling skills. They have discretion, within predefined limits, to offer service recovery gestures. If they cannot resolve the complaint they escalate it to the central team at Nokia Group. Staff are encouraged not to worry about the cost of complaint resolution or recapturing loyalty. They are trained to use a five-step process for fixing problems:

1 Listen from the customer's perspective.

2 Create a solution.

3 Execute improvement (try new things, not seen as a failure but learning).

4 Ensure an excellent recovery process.

5 Build 'wow' experiences.

A useful way of looking at return on investment in terms of complaints is to use customer satisfaction data and other management information you may have available in your organization to quantify the negative impact of not dealing with complaints well.

For example, you can:

- identify the percentage of customers who do complain (even though these potentially represent the tip of the iceberg);
- look at how many of the people who did complain were not satisfied with the way their complaint was dealt with;

- identify the negative actions customers take as a result, such as ending their relationship with you, not taking up other products and services, or negative word of mouth, and the cost to you of such actions.

In the following chapters I will provide practical examples of how to encourage and respond effectively to complaints, as well as how to act on customer feedback to ensure ongoing improvement.

Ultimately people who handle complaints need to represent the ears, eyes and hearts of your customers. By managing and learning from complaints, you can drive improvements in your overall customer experience.

Key learning points

- By welcoming complaints and dealing with them efficiently, thoroughly and fairly, organizations are able to deliver a superior customer experience.

- Effective complaint management helps drive improvements in products, services and processes.

- It also encourages better employee morale and engagement, as team members can use complaints to represent the voice of the customer and see that actions are taken to improve the organization as a result of customer feedback.

- Finally, dealing with complaints well delivers strong and sustainable profitable growth, by increasing customer loyalty and retention and generating an enviable reputation for great service.

Rate your organization's approach to complaint handling

Having read this chapter, consider how well your organization manages complaints. Look at the following statements and provide a rating to indicate your agreement on a scale of 1 to 10 to each of the following questions, where 1 = No, I do not agree, we never do this and 10 = Yes, I totally agree, we always do this.

1. Senior managers in our organization welcome complaints and see them as a positive way to improve.   Your score: ___

2. We make it easy for our customers to complain to us via whatever channel they choose.   Your score: ___

3. Our employees treat complaints seriously.   Your score: ___

4. Employees are given adequate training in how to deal with complaints.   Your score: ___

5. The process we use to deal with complaints is timely and effective.   Your score: ___

6. Our employees record all the complaints they receive.   Your score: ___

7. We thoroughly investigate complaints and provide a timely and fair response to customers.   Your score: ___

8. The organization uses complaint data to drive improvements across the business.   Your score: ___

9. I can name at least one improvement action that has been taken as a result of a complaint we have received.   Your score: ___

10. My organization views complaint management as an investment in the future of the business rather than a cost.   Your score: ___

Now review your scores. Use the chapters that follow in this book to identify actions you can take to areas where you have scored 7 or less.

Encouraging dissatisfied customers to voice their complaints

02

In this chapter I look at:

- why customers do not always complain;
- ways to encourage people to complain;
- making best use of social media;
- the regulatory environment.

Like the previous chapter, this one ends with a check list that allows you to assess your organization's strengths and weaknesses in this area.

Encouraging complaints

As we have seen in the previous chapter, people who do complain to an organization are giving it the chance to put things right. However, we have also seen that many people do not complain directly to a service provider but tell other people of their bad experience, either in person or online.

Logic says that if an organization can encourage dissatisfied customers to complain, the more chance it has to create customer advocacy and loyalty.

However, first the organization needs to understand why customers do not always complain.

Why customers do not complain

A recent survey conducted in the UK by my company, The Stairway Consultancy, found that there were four main reasons why customers who were dissatisfied with a product or service they had received did not complain to the organization concerned. Figure 2.1 illustrates these four factors:

● Customers did not think anything would happen as a result of complaining.

● Complaining was too much hassle.

● Customers found it difficult to reach the right department.

● They did not have time to complain.

The fact that one in two dissatisfied customers who did not complain were prevented from doing so because they felt that nothing would happen is worrying; it demonstrates a general mistrust of companies and belief that they will not listen or act on customer feedback. In a subsequent question in

FIGURE 2.1 Principal reasons why customers had not complained

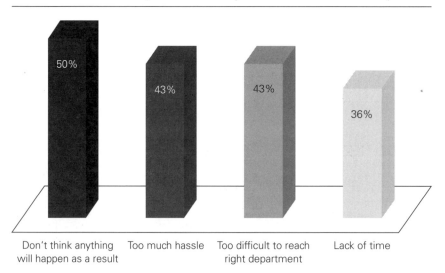

Don't think anything will happen as a result	Too much hassle	Too difficult to reach right department	Lack of time

NOTE: the percentages are not mutually exclusive, so for example respondents may have answered both 'lack of time' and 'too much hassle'.

the survey, we asked customers who had not complained what would have encouraged them to do so. Most, 64 per cent, told us that knowing it would have made a difference would have done so, while 36 per cent cited knowing who to complain to and 29 per cent spoke of receiving a quick response (Figure 2.2).

Clearly businesses need to do more to publicize what they have learnt and the actions they have taken as a result of complaints, as this would increase consumer confidence that it is worth complaining.

Doing a search of best-practice customer-service websites, I have found companies who publish the details of the number of complaints that they receive, especially those businesses that operate in a regulatory environment. However, it is rare to find websites that publicize the actions that companies have taken as a result of complaints. The exceptions in the UK appear to be some government organizations that provide a 'You Said, We Did' section on their websites, thereby being transparent about what has happened as a result of complaints. Barclays Bank provides an online newsletter that

FIGURE 2.2 What would encourage customers who had not complained to complain

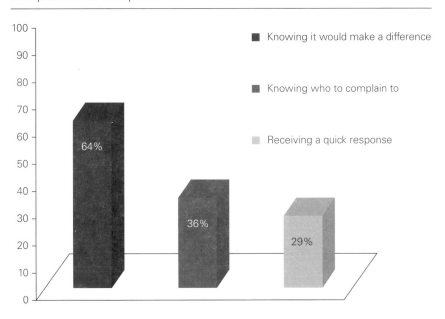

NOTE: the percentages are not mutually exclusive.

summarizes the improvement actions it has taken as a result of customer feedback. For example, in a recent edition it stated: 'We now accept Online Statements for residential and buy-to-let mortgage applications and you won't have to get them stamped by your bank first.'

Ways to encourage people to complain

All organizations need customers to tell them when they are unhappy with their products and service so they can understand where they are going wrong and do something about it. Our research indicates that there are three key actions that organizations need to take to encourage people to complain:

- publicize ways to complain;
- respond to complaints quickly;
- publicize improvement actions.

Publicize ways to complain

Ensure your complaint processes are well publicized, clear and easily accessible to customers via their preferred form of communication.

For example, in the UK the pharmacy company Boots sets out its complaints procedure on its website in the following way:

Our aim is to provide excellent service at all times. If we fail to reach these standards and you are unhappy with our prescription or pharmacy service in any way, you can speak to a member of our pharmacy team or the pharmacist in charge by calling 0845 121 9040.

If your concerns are not fully addressed by this you may wish to formalize your complaint in one of the following ways:

- By telephoning Boots Customer Care on 0845 0708090

- By writing with your complaint to: Boots Customer Care, P O Box 5300, Nottingham, NG90 1AA

- By complaining by e-mail to **customerservice@care.boots.com**

However, it does not set out anticipated response times to manage customer expectations.

The online retailer Amazon publicizes its customer-service facility under the Help section of its website which states that customers can contact the company via e-mail or phone, but does not explicitly set out how people can complain.

The online and telephone banking service first direct, on the other hand, explains on its website the ways people can complain and the three-step escalation process, as well as the timescales in which it will reply to complaints:

Your views are important to us. If we do not deliver the standard of service you expect, or if we make a mistake, we want to know. We will investigate the situation and set about putting things right as quickly as possible. Where appropriate, we will also take steps to avoid making similar mistakes in the future.

We hope that you will never need to progress beyond the first step. However, we wish to give you every opportunity to present your case where you remain unsatisfied.

Step 1

Contact us and provide us with the details of your complaint. Where possible, we will try to give you an answer there and then. If not, we will take full details from you and arrange for the problem to be investigated. We will respond to you within five business weekdays. Where a full response is not possible at this stage, we will contact you and advise you how long our investigations are likely to take.

Step 2

In the unlikely event that your complaint is not resolved to your satisfaction you can contact the Manager of the department concerned:

By telephone:	**08 456 100 100** (**08 456 100 147** textphone) (International number **+44 113 2345678**)
By e-mail:	via secure message on Internet Banking. Select 'contact us' and then 'secure message' from the left hand menu and then choose 'dissatisfied'.
In writing:	Customer Relations **first direct** 40 Wakefield Road Leeds LS98 1FD

We will issue you with a response within five business weekdays. Where a full response is not possible at this stage, we will contact you and advise you how long our investigations are likely to take.

Step 3

Our aim is to resolve all your concerns internally. However, if you are not satisfied with our final response, or if eight weeks have passed since you first raised your complaint with us, you have the right to refer your complaint to the FOS.

You can write to:
Financial Ombudsman Service
South Quay Plaza
183 Marsh Wall
London
E14 9SR

By telephone:	0845 080 1800
By e-mail:	**complaint.info@financial-ombudsman.org.uk** (or simply log-on to their website at **www.financial-ombudsman.org.uk**)

We intend to resolve your concerns fairly and quickly. In most cases this can be done if you allow the department involved to listen to your concerns, understand the problem and then deliver an effective solution to you.

First direct also has a section on its website called the first direct Lab where existing customers and members of the public can view new ideas and test-drive innovations before they are released.

Self-service options are also becoming more popular with consumers. For example Virgin Airlines has an online help facility where customers can ask a question or request help and get an instant reply. Low-cost airline AirAsia actively encourages live chat with the slogan: 'Hate the call centre? Ask me for answers.' The company's owner comes up with an answer in the box when you type in your question (although in reality the system uses semantic analysis and self-learning to extract the meaning from the question and provide one of 20,000 replies).

Check that your customers are able to complain via whatever channel they choose, be it face to face or via:

- e-mail;
- letter;
- phone;
- website;
- call-back option online;
- online help;
- a response via social media channels such as Twitter, Facebook and LinkedIn.

Respond to complaints quickly

One of the reasons that customers fail to complain when they are dissatisfied is the perception that they will not receive a speedy reply. In this fast-paced world, customers expect to be able to reach you 24/7 and for you to resolve their complaint on the very first call or at least within a day. In a survey by Aspect Customer Service Trends 2011, 70 per cent of respondents who reported that they were 'very satisfied' or 'satisfied' said their problem was resolved on the first or second attempt, and 40 per cent of those who were 'dissatisfied' or 'very dissatisfied' said their problem resolution took longer.

The expectation of speed of response is putting increasing pressure on companies' infrastructure, and in many cases is unrealistic. How businesses manage customers' expectations in relation to timescales for resolving complaints is an issue I will discuss in more depth later in the book.

Publicize improvement actions

When customers do not hear of any positive improvement as a result of their complaints, they lose confidence and trust in an organization. As our research shows, many customers do not believe it is worth voicing their dissatisfaction as no action will be taken.

It is important, from both an employee and a customer perspective, to publicize what improvements you have made as a result of complaints. Thanet District Council in the UK, for example, has a 'You Said, We Did' page on its website listing the actions that it has taken as a result of complaints and suggestions.

Making best use of social media

I recently had to purchase car insurance in France and had little knowledge of the companies involved. I went on an internet forum to find out what customers were saying about the range of insurance companies I had shortlisted, and which had fewest complaints, before I made a decision about where to buy. I know of many other people who use community forums to identify best-practice organizations as a customer. It is tempting to dismiss social media as a young people's medium. However, this is a growing way for customers to express their dissatisfaction to their peers and other potential customers.

Social media are any media that are generated by customers. The term includes Facebook, Twitter, Google Plus, MySpace, YouTube and LinkedIn but also covers blogs, message boards, product review sites and aggregators such as TripAdvisor. What defines social media is that it is ubiquitous and it is immediate. Customer-to-customer support is on the rise. Many people now pay more attention to other customers' reports on a product and service rather than trusting the marketing blurb issued by a company. The customer community itself is often far larger than your employee population and, perhaps unlike all your employees, the customer community has direct experience of your products and services. It is like a giant global customer focus group, where the organization cannot control the questions or the answers. It makes complaining easier and more transparent to all consumers. It also requires a careful response from companies to manage the issues that customers raise online.

The food giant Nestlé fell foul of social media when it tried to stop a co-ordinated series of complaints from Greenpeace activists who protested against the company's use of palm oil. Nestlé tried to fight the criticism by censoring its Facebook site, which resulted in increased negative publicity and attack.

One musician, a customer of United Airlines, discovered that his $3,500 Taylor guitar was damaged during baggage handling on a flight. After nine months of trying to get someone at the airline to take responsibility for his complaint, the customer wrote a song about his frustrating experience and also created a music video that he posted on YouTube. The video amassed 5 million viewings within one month and was a public relations disaster for United, which finally offered compensation for the broken guitar.

Domino's Pizza on the other hand effectively used social media to counter complaints it had received from customers about the quality of its pizzas. It created a microsite and posted videos on YouTube showing the improvements that its chefs had made to its recipes as a result of customer feedback. Domino's then invited feedback from its customers on the new pizza.

Coffee chain Starbucks actively seeks customers' opinions, compliments and criticisms on its website. It has set up a section that is called My Starbucks Idea that has netted tens of thousands of ideas, some of which were implemented, such as free birthday drinks.

Social media are altering customers' expectations about service as well as their buying patterns. Take a few moments to put your company name in a search engine. What you will find is all the forums and blogs that relate to your company, and what customers are saying about you. It is also worthwhile putting the word 'sucks' after your company name in a search engine and see what appears. Visit the numerous complaint websites that have sprung up that allow customers to post their dissatisfaction and compare notes with other people. You will start to appreciate how online reports can go viral and reach millions of people in a short space of time.

I predict a time when calling a company's contact centre will no longer be the fastest way to have a complaint resolved. Tweeting your complaint or putting it on Facebook may obtain a quicker response. One Comcast cable customer for example tweeted his dissatisfaction when he turned on the TV to watch an important match and instead found an old sitcom on their channel. Comcast's head of digital care saw the tweet and immediately tweeted back to the customer and other tweeters that the problem was caused by a power failure at the match that meant that the company had to show the sitcom instead.

In 2005 a blogger set up a posting about computer company Dell under the title 'Dell Hell'. This created a massive amount of bad publicity for the firm. Since then, Dell has placed great emphasis on having conversations with customers via social media. It has a team of people trawling the web to answer issues raised by dissatisfied customers. Its social media team manages its Twitter accounts and Facebook pages as well as Dell's customer forum, called IdeaStorm. The forum has generated over 100,000 customer comments in four years. Customers have put forward 16,000 ideas to Dell, which has implemented close to 500 of them. This technique is called 'crowdsourcing' and is on the increase across the globe. (Crowdsourcing refers to the fact that any comment or posting on the internet is visible to all and may be responded to online by a crowd.) If the ideas generated by consumers produce something great for Dell, that's a major win, but the main benefit is having consumers feel that they're part of the process.

If you have not done so already, it is time to incorporate these unsolicited service channels into your complaint operating procedures. There is customized software available to allow businesses to insert a customer's name or e-mail address and see which social media the customer uses. A piece of software called 'tweetscan' will tell you what conversations your customers are having about you. Other organizations are building online communities to facilitate conversations with their customers. One software provider, Get Satisfaction, estimates that over 50,000 companies use its product to provide a social support experience to listen and talk to their customers. There is software also available to integrate social media sites such as Facebook with an organization's website and customer-service centre. Text analysis also allows you to analyse the voice of the customer via different listening posts such as contact centres, customer e-mails and blogs so that you can identify key customer concerns.

Southwest Airlines in the United States, like other businesses, has a social media team dedicated to answering complaints online. This includes a 'Chief Twitter Officer'. In the United States – and gradually in places like the UK, Australia and Canada – complaint-handling teams are beginning to monitor and respond to complaints via social media channels. Telecoms giants BT in the UK and AT&T in the United States have social media teams who monitor and respond to customer comments. BT learnt to its cost how powerful social media can be when the celebrity Lily Allen posted a tweet on Twitter complaining about the poor service of BT, her internet provider, and asking if anyone had the contact details of BT's chief executive.

Research indicates that a negative review or comment by a frustrated and dissatisfied customer on social media channels can lose companies as many as 30 other customers. The impact of a negative review by a celebrity can be far greater. Lily Allen has over 3 million followers on Twitter and BT was forced to respond quickly to dampen the subsequent furore. In the UK, BT is using specially developed software to scan for negative comments about it on social media sites including Twitter, Facebook and YouTube, as are companies such as phone retailer Carphone Warehouse, banks including Lloyds TSB and budget airline easyJet. Complainants are then contacted by e-mail suggesting ways the company can help to solve the problem.

However, privacy campaigners have voiced concern about the practice, and have accused firms of 'spying' on their customers. Legal experts have also raised the issue of data protection law if a company approaches a customer in an unsolicited manner. However, the firms involved claim there is nothing sinister about the practice, and the key point is that they are only looking at what people are talking about in public spaces.

Double deviation

Social media are becoming an enormously powerful way for those organizations that embrace them positively to build customer advocacy. Customers who have complained and whose complaints have been dealt with well are the most credible to other customers. Social media should therefore be built into the spread of communication channels that organizations use so as to encourage customers who are dissatisfied to voice their complaint.

However, I believe that the key to handling complaints well is to respond speedily to the customers via whatever channel they prefer. Ironically, many of the comments on BT's own Twitter page are written by customers complaining they are not able to reach BT call-centre staff by phone. Interestingly a report in *MIT Sloan Management Review* by Thomas M Tripp and Yany Gregoire (Spring 2011) shows that complaining publicly online almost always follows what the authors call a 'double deviation'. Tripp and Gregoire analysed 431 complaints posted in the United States on two websites: consumeraffairs.com and ripoffreport.com. They found that 96 per cent of the people who had posted the complaints online had experienced a series of failed resolution attempts via other channels. Typically these customers had already complained via more traditional channels to the organization.

Frustrated to the point of anger that the service provider did not resolve their complaint or demonstrate that they wanted to preserve their loyalty, the customers turned to social networks to vent their annoyance.

'Double deviation' refers to the fact that the service provider has not only deviated from delivering a service that the customer expected in the first place, it has then also deviated from best practice by ignoring the customer's complaint. The study also found that such customers feel 'betrayed' by the organization and therefore justified in using every means to 'get even'. Customers are more likely to complain via social networks after experiencing a double deviation around a serious service or product failure that they cannot ignore, such as car or financial problems.

Within my own family, one family member was angry at a major car manufacturer's response to his complaint about the spare wheel on his car that kept falling off because the wheel nuts that attached it to the underside of the car were faulty. Having lost three spare wheels because of this and having repeatedly complained without success, he set up a microsite to publicize and provide a warning about the problem to other customers.

I am conscious even as I write this that the use of social media is on the rise, and by the time you read this there may have been even more changes. The key therefore is to monitor what is happening and to be proactive. You can even head off potential problems in this way. In December 2010 there was unprecedented heavy snow in many parts of Southern England. Local authorities came under increasing criticism about their lack of speedy response to the poor weather conditions. One council, Windsor and Maidenhead, however, received praise for its effective use of Twitter, tweeting where the gritting lorries were working and keeping customers constantly updated about their progress throughout the bad weather.

In responding to customers who complain online, speed is of the essence. Customers whose complaints are not dealt with speedily and fairly will seek to avoid the company permanently and continue to hold a grudge, even though their wish for revenge may fade over time.

Although the use of social media is on the rise, more than 75 per cent of complaints are still made over the telephone. Studies show that for now voice remains the preferred channel because speed of response is essential for today's consumers. Be mindful that as more complaint departments respond to complaints via social media channels, this preference is likely to change.

To demonstrate how impressed customers can be when they make a complaint over the internet and it is dealt with speedily, here is a comment on a US blog (**www.dfc.com/blog/?p=13**) from Debbie, a customer of OtterBox:

Yesterday evening (*Mar 1*) I dropped my Blackberry Torch on the carpet in my bedroom. As I felt my phone drop I wasn't particularly worried because I encased my precious Blackberry in an Otterbox. This commuter series Otter Box caresses my Blackberry in silicone rubber and then covers that with some sort of impact resistant plastic; so dropping the Torch is usually no big deal. However, last night when my phone dropped on the carpet – and came out safe and sound – part of the Otter broke and came off of my Torch. Imagine my surprise that this happened on a carpet!

As I had bought this Otter at Costco, I figured I would just take it back and whine... but I bought it in October of 2010. Costco has a 90-day return policy. I went to **www.otterbox.com** and found that Otter offers a one-year warranty. As it was 10:27 pm (note the time) I sent an e-mail to customer service, not expecting a reply for a day or two. Imagine my surprise when I received a very nice e-mail from Amanda at 10:29 pm expressing her disappointment that I wasn't totally happy with their product. She offered to send me replacement if I sent her the color of the case, my contact information and a phone number with which to reach me. I immediately replied to Amanda which went out at 10:34 pm and at 10:40 pm she replied that the order for my replacement had been placed! I received an e-mail from OtterBox at 10:39 pm indicating that my order had been placed and was being processed. Imagine, in a little more than 10 *minutes* my broken OtterBox had gone from a inquiry to customer service all the way to a complete no-charge replacement with minimal effort on my part!

The regulatory environment

The complaint-management environment is increasingly affected by legislation and sector regulations. Be mindful therefore of the regulatory environment in which you operate. Across the globe as customer empowerment increases, governments have put in place regulators to ensure that customers are being treated fairly. These are prevalent in marketplaces where customer service is a mature industry, and are likely to increase in emerging marketplaces.

One of my biggest frustrations where firms are regulated is that complaint handling is often seen as just a regulatory requirement, another area where organizations need to be compliant. People tend to forget that the regulations are there to protect the consumer, and that ultimately great complaint handling leads to customer loyalty and retention. For example, in the UK as elsewhere, the financial services industry is regulated. A Key Note report in 2010 entitled Customer Services in Financial Organisations: Market Assessment 2010 revealed that 57 per cent of consumers surveyed felt that financial services providers do not care about their customers. This is in spite of the regulator having set out a policy that all firms need to adhere to called 'Treating customers fairly' and DISP (dispute resolution) rules relating to complaints.

Regulators will vary by market sector and location. However, if you do work in a regulated environment such as telecoms, utilities or financial services, then most regulators will not only issue best-practice guidelines for dealing with complaints but also have the power to monitor complaint handling and to impose penalties for non-compliance. They also provide benchmark data and encourage the sharing of best practice.

To deliver a truly excellent customer experience, firms need to meet or exceed any legal, regulatory or voluntary code or independent arbitration service requirements relating to complaints. View any regulatory requirements as a minimum standard that you should always seek to exceed. Look beyond the potential cost of non-compliance and recognize the benefits of effective complaint management to the overall customer experience.

Complaints standards bodies

Just as regulations and legislation is on the increase in complaint management, so are the number of complaint-management standards. The British Standards Institution, Standards Australia and the Argentinian Standards Organization have all developed complaints-handling standards. Standards Australia has also developed a guide to preventing, handling and resolving disputes.

The International Organization for Standardization standard ISO 10002:2004 is the internationally recognized standard on complaints handling. Many organizations across the world, from Mumbai International Airport in India to mobile services company Mobinil in Egypt, have attained accreditation. The standard sets out guidelines for the development and implementation of effective complaint management. It emphasizes the need for fair, transparent, efficient processes operated by well-trained employees. It also advocates tracking and monitoring complaints and a process of continuous improvement.

Organizations such as my own have built a complaints-handling approach into the company's overall approach to quality management, by adopting the ISO 9000 quality-management system.

Key learning points

- Complaints are free feedback! Encourage customers who are dissatisfied to voice their concerns via whatever channel is convenient to them.

- Publicize widely how customers can voice their dissatisfaction.

- Respond quickly to complaints, at the same time ensuring you undertake a thorough investigation.

- Publicize improvement actions so all your customers can see.

- Monitor social networking sites for complaints and respond accordingly. Customers believe what your customers say about your company more than any of your own paid advertising.

- If you are working in a regulated environment, ensure that you meet or exceed any requirements relating to complaints.

- International complaint-management and quality-management systems can provide useful standards for complaint handling.

Rate how well your organization encourages customers who are dissatisfied to complain

Having read this chapter, consider how well your organization encourages customers to voice their complaints. Look at the following statements and provide a rating to indicate your agreement on a scale of 1 to 10 to each of the following questions, where 1 = 'No, I do not agree, we never do this' and '10 = Yes, I totally agree, we always do this'.

1. We publicize widely to consumers how they can complain if they are dissatisfied with our service.   Your score: ___

2. Our customers are able to complain via whatever channel they choose be it:
   e-mail
   letter
   phone
   website
   call back option online
   online help
   face to face
   via social media channels such as Twitter, Facebook and LinkedIn.   Your score: ___

3. We have dedicated resource to monitor and respond to complaints made via social media channels.   Your score: ___

4. We respond quickly and thoroughly to complaints.   Your score: ___

5. We publicize to customers the improvement actions that we have taken as a result of learning from complaints.   Your score: ___

6. We meet the standards required by the regulator if we work in a regulated environment.   Your score: ___

What people look for when they complain

03

In this chapter I look at:

- the key priorities for customers when they complain;
- how well businesses are meeting their expectations;
- financial compensation and other forms of redress.

I also provide a checklist so that you can rate how well your organization addresses customers' needs.

What is important to customers when they complain?

I recently had cause to complain to my bank about a cheque that had been cashed for the wrong amount. I had made it out to a window cleaner for £54, only to discover that it had gone through my account as £5,400! Naturally I was alarmed and called straight away to complain. I, like most customers who complain, was looking for a speedy resolution and for my complaint to be taken seriously. I wanted a refund of my money, an apology and to be treated with empathy.

The bank concerned admitted that they had made a keying error and offered to redress the situation that day. Unfortunately they then failed to follow through on their promises and it took another two weeks to refund my money!

FIGURE 3.1 What customers look for when they complain

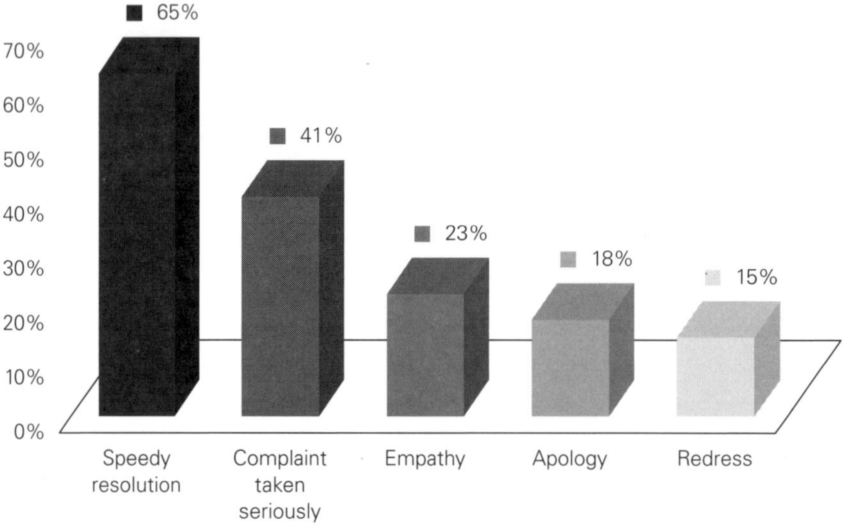

NOTE: the figures are not mutually exclusive.

Figure 3.1 shows the results of The Stairway Consultancy's research about what people look for when they complain. I will discuss financial and non-financial redress later in this chapter, but first let us focus on the key customer requirement of a speedy resolution, which two out of three of our respondents put at the top of their expectations.

Fast resolutions to complaints

As I have mentioned earlier, we live in a fast-moving society where people expect to receive service 24/7. Customers require swift resolutions to their complaints and want to deal with businesses that quickly put things right. When we asked complainants about the timescale they expected for a speedy resolution, 80 per cent of respondents said they wanted one within 24 hours. In fact further studies show that the longer it takes for an organization to respond to a complaint, the less satisfied the complainant is with the outcome.

From an organization's perspective, is it possible to resolve a complaint within 24 hours? Potentially the answer is no, unless the complaint is of a very simple nature. One of the dangers of resolving complaints quickly is that the business may not investigate the complaint thoroughly and therefore may not arrive at a fair outcome for the customer. I know of at least one company that adopted this approach, only for the industry regulator to tell them to re-open their cases because the resolutions they had proposed to their customers could not be supported with evidence.

Call the customer

One of the key learning points for managing complaints, therefore, is to manage the customer's expectation of how long the complaint will take to resolve. When I called my bank and was told that the complaint would be remedied that day I expected this to happen, and when it did not I was disappointed.

Best-practice organizations make speedy contact with the customer by phone as soon as they receive a complaint. In fact research shows that 70 per cent of customers would like to be contacted by phone, whatever channel they use to complain. The benefit of doing this is that the customers know that their complaint is being taken seriously and they have a personal, named contact from the organization who is dealing with their complaint. In addition they have an opportunity to explain more about the circumstances of their complaint. The person calling the customer from the company also has an opportunity to manage the customer's expectations about how long the complaint will take to thoroughly investigate and resolve.

How fast can we reasonably expect a company to investigate a complaint? This depends on the complexity of the complaint itself and the amount of resource the company has to resolve the issue. I believe that investigating complaints should be given priority over other work, irrespective of whether the organization has a centralized, dedicated complaint-handling department.

Some regulated industries, such as financial services in the UK, have a cut-off point (in this instance eight weeks) after which a complainant can go to independent arbitration if a complaint is not resolved. Consider setting benchmarks in terms of thorough investigation and resolution of complaints. For example, targeting your business to resolve 80 per cent of complaints within a month and 99 per cent within two months if you want to deliver a high level of customer experience. Whatever your timescale, it is important to keep customers informed about the progress of your investigations.

Single deviation

In the last chapter I spoke about 'double deviation', where customers spread negative criticism about a company on the internet as a result of failure to resolve their issue in the first place.

Customers who complain are giving an organization a chance to put things right. However, the organization only has one chance to do this well. Forty-four per cent of customers give a business only two chances to rectify a problem before taking their business elsewhere.

Failing to deliver on promises or managing customer expectations – as in the case of the £5,400 I expected to be credited to my account – falls into the category of 'double deviation'. Customers who complain are far more unforgiving if two things go wrong. My advice is to train your employees to 'get it right first time'. Later in this book I talk about the need for competent and trained staff who deal with complaints quickly and fairly, and for making sure they have collected the right information to prevent any mistakes happening again.

Taking complaints seriously

Following a complaint the most important thing that would make a customer consider changing from one company to another is indifference from the company's customer-service personnel. Therefore, the most important thing an organization should be doing when receiving a complaint from the customer is making the customer feel valued.

When I took my car in to have new tyres fixed recently, I left it with the garage for the day so they could complete the job. I was dismayed to find on my return that the keys to my car were missing. The garage said that they had misplaced them somewhere and could not find them. They advised me to return home and get my second set of spare keys so that I could pick up the vehicle. Despite the garage admitting they had lost the keys and knowing that this was a security risk and could potentially invalidate my insurance, the people I dealt with did not take my complaint seriously. I had no option but to use my spare keys to return home and phone each day to see if they had found the keys. After a week, still no one was interested in helping me and I eventually escalated my complaint to the area manager. My level of frustration and annoyance increased steadily each day.

One of the key behaviours I wanted was for the company to be interested in my complaint and to take any expression of dissatisfaction seriously. Research shows this is true for many other customers.

The emotional and economic cost of complaints

Every time customers complain, they incur two costs: both the economic cost of complaining and the emotional cost.

From an economic perspective, customers invest time and effort in having to complain. In certain circumstances they also incur costs. In addition, when things go wrong for the customer there is the emotional cost that the situation evokes. Typically a complaint provokes distress and inconvenience. The emotions that this evokes in the customer could be, for example, disappointment, annoyance and frustration. If the customer's complaint is very serious or if the complaint is not dealt with well, this can also provoke anger. Often the customer's emotional state can cloud the rational way in which they deal with the company that caused them to complain.

For example, with my garage, the more the people I spoke to did not take my complaint seriously, the more incensed I became about the situation and the more determined I was to have the garage put things right.

Companies that do not recognize the emotional cost of complaining and fail to train their staff to recognize it run the risk of resolving an issue with a customer, but not engendering loyalty.

Loyalty is an emotional connection that we have with a person or a business. From a psychological perspective, loyalty is also about trust. Difficult situations test trust and tell us much about the quality and nature of our bond with the organization. When a business goes out of its way to understand the customer's situation and put things right when things have gone wrong, it makes customers trust them more, and as a consequence feel more loyal.

A study of consumer emotions by SOCAP in Australia found that 'on the whole, failing to meet expectations does much more harm than exceeding expectations does good.' When customers who complained had their complaints handled well, they reported feeling reassured, relieved, grateful and impressed. The study concluded that those who had a less than satisfactory experience when making a complaint were unlikely to re-establish a trusting relationship with the organization.

Empathy and apology

What was missing for me in the way that the garage treated me was a sense of empathy and understanding of my situation. I was seriously concerned that someone at the garage had stolen my keys, knew where I lived and was likely to steal my car, which would not be insured as I had entrusted the keys to the garage.

The Stairway research into what people look for when they complain indicates that empathy and apology are two key behaviours that customers expect. In my garage example, I needed the staff with whom I discussed the situation to put themselves in my shoes and to demonstrate that they understood my predicament. I also wanted someone to say sorry that the situation had arisen, even if they were not prepared to admit their mistake.

I discuss more later in the book about both of these key skills and how to apply them.

Meeting expectations

So how well do businesses meet customers' expectations about the way that their complaints are dealt with?

In our study, the top four expectations of customers who had complained were:

- speedy resolution;
- complaint taken seriously;
- empathy;
- apology.

FIGURE 3.2 The difference between what customers expected when they complained and how they were treated

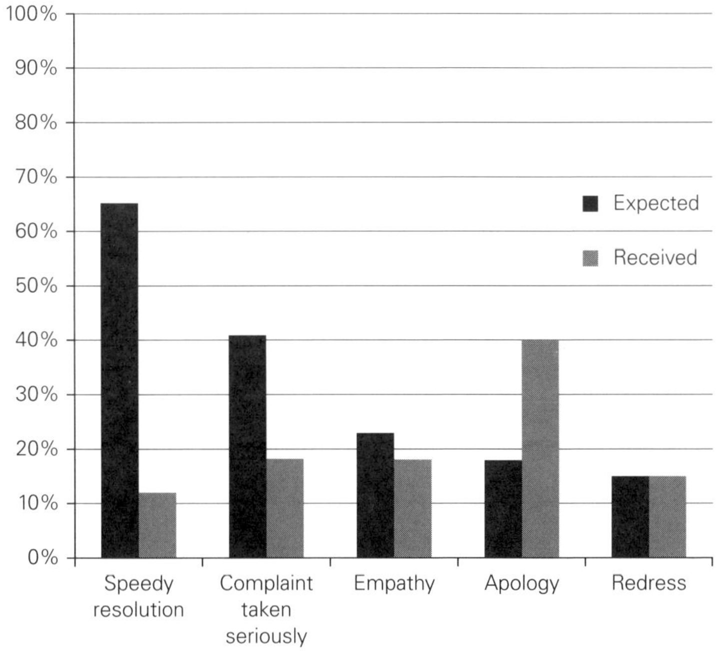

NOTE: the figures are not mutually exclusive.

Figure 3.2 illustrates respondents' actual experience of a complaint and how well they were treated in relation to their expectations.

The findings show that in our sample customers did receive an apology more often than they expected, which is a positive. However, there were large gaps between customers' expectations of the speed of response and how long their complaint took to resolve. In addition customers reported they were not happy that their complaints were not taken seriously. This indicates that there is a lack of customer focus in many companies.

Overall in our survey 36 per cent of respondents rated the way that their complaint had been handled as 'poor' or 'very poor'. Whilst just over half (54 per cent) were satisfied with the way their complaint was dealt with, only 9 per cent rated it 'very good' and 1 per cent 'excellent', implying that there is much room for improvement.

What makes best-in-class complaint handling?

The respondents in our study who did rate the way that their complaint was dealt with as positive cited the following reasons:

- They made it clear they understood the problem.
- They listened, understood and acted promptly.
- They took me seriously when I said I was unhappy.
- They addressed all the issues.
- They gave me a fast response.

Conversely, those who were not happy with the way that their complaint was dealt with cited examples such as:

- It took a very long time to resolve.
- They said they had sorted the problem out and in fact they had not; I needed to complain again.
- It took contact with a number of different departments to get fully resolved.

When asked what companies could do to better manage complaints, typical responses were:

- Provide a speedier resolution. Pick up the phone to deal with the situation rather than dealing with everything in writing.
- Listen and be more flexible in understanding my personal situation.
- Delve deeper. Track the complaint more thoroughly.
- Provide more information on correct contact points. Make it clearer who to complain to.
- Deal with the whole situation in one go – it took several attempts to get resolved.
- Take responsibility for following through on their promises. More staff empowerment to make quicker decisions.
- Provide easier access to management. Less red tape.
- Be prepared to admit they are wrong.
- Take the issue more seriously in the first place and do what they said they would do.
- State what they would be looking to change in the future as a result.

So customers want service providers to take their complaints seriously and to provide a speedy and thorough resolution to their complaint. They want the knowledge that action has been taken as a result of their complaint. Later I will discuss staff empowerment and the role managers need to take in dealing with complaints.

What about money?

You will notice that our research findings indicate that only the minority of customers expect financial compensation (redress) as a result of their complaint. This was 15 per cent of people in our survey. As the study shows, showing empathy and saying sorry are often more important to customers.

Redress is the general term to describe financial and non-financial payments and tokens given to customers as the result of a complaint. One of the difficulties complaints professionals often come across is deciding the level of redress, if any, that should be given to a customer.

There is often a tendency for members of staff to think they are saving the organization money if they do not offer redress to customers. Yet people should remember that complaint management is an investment in customer loyalty and retention rather than a cost. If redress is appropriate, depending on the individual circumstances of the complaint, then it is better to recognize this in a fair manner and maintain the customer's trust.

Different countries and different regulators have guidelines about what is appropriate to give in terms of redress. However, the overriding sentiment is that if the customer makes a complaint and the organization is at fault, it should return the customer to the position he or she would have been in if the error had not occurred. In addition complaint handlers should take into account the degree of emotional distress and inconvenience that the customer has suffered.

What to consider when offering redress

Your organization probably has guidance that you can refer to about similar types of common complaints and what has been done in the past.

Importantly, each complainant's circumstance will be different and I would caution organizations against applying a blanket approach to redress. The complaint handler needs to assess how the customer has been affected by the problem from both an economic and an emotional point of view. Best practice is to ask the customer what would resolve the complaint for them. It could be that a simple apology and admission of error may be all that they are looking for.

Key is to treat each customer as an individual and to apply redress fairly. I have worked with organizations where those who shout loudest get the highest level of financial payment as a result of a complaint. This is not fair on other customers who may not have the same power and influence. Likewise, I have seen firms that attempt to negotiate with customers around the levels of financial redress they will give. They typically start at a low offer and only increase this if the customer will not accept it. Again negotiation is not an option if you want to treat your customers honestly and fairly, and I strongly recommend avoiding this approach.

Likewise, I would always take the customer's word, unless I have evidence to show otherwise, about how much time or money they have spent in attempting to resolve the complaint. Asking for receipts in most cases, unless very large amounts are involved, puts barriers up to customers and implies that you do not trust them. Why penalize the 99 per cent of the customers who complain and to whom a redress payment is justified, just to deter the 1 per cent of customers whose claim to financial redress may be fraudulent?

Types of financial and non-financial redress

If you have made an error and uphold the customer's complaint, you have four options about how to recompense them, depending on the circumstances. These are:

- replace or exchange;
- reimburse;
- refund;
- compensate.

If you are a bricks-and-mortar or an online retailer, one of the most useful forms of redress is to offer a replacement of goods or an exchange. Marks & Spencer was one of the first retailers in the UK to offer a 'no quibbles' exchange or refund (see below) policy. As a consequence it built an enviable reputation for excellent customer service.

Another form of redress is reimbursements. These are payments to cover the external costs incurred by the customer as a result of the organization's error. So for example, when I complained that the garage had lost my car keys, I had to get a taxi to my home and back to pick up my spare keys. When my complaint was finally resolved, the garage reimbursed my travel costs and the cost of my telephone calls to the company to sort out the situation. Reimbursements include third-party expenses as well as travel expenses and the cost of telephone calls.

There may be circumstances where the organization needs to make a refund to the customer as a result of their complaint. The purpose of a refund is to return the customer to the position he or she would have been in had the error not occurred. So, when I complained to my bank about the cheque about a £54 cheque being cashed for £5,400 as a result of bank error, I needed to be refunded the money. I also needed to be refunded the interest I would have accrued on the £5,400 that the bank took from my account in error.

A further option if the complaint is justified and the organization has made an error is to offer the customer compensation. This can be a financial payment or a gift to the customer in acknowledgement of the inconvenience or distress the complaint situation has caused.

The level of compensation you choose to offer customers depends on the degree of emotional cost and the impact on them of the complaint situation. For some people money is not appropriate as compensation and it may be more appropriate to send a gift of flowers, wine or chocolates or a donation to charity. Many companies – like financial services provider Nationwide – have a range of non-financial token and gifts that their complaint handlers can select to send to a customer. Careful consideration should be given to send the appropriate token as compensation – it would cause more problems, for example, to send a gift of wine to a teetotaller!

To ensure sufficient action is taken to fix any problems, Federal Express's (FedEx) Customer Satisfaction Policy states that staff should:

- take any step to solve customer problems;
- arrange the most expeditious delivery;
- provide prompt refund or credits when FedEx fails the customer.

Reinforcing this, FedEx has established clear reimbursement and empowerment standards for different job levels and functions. These enable phone representatives to refund up to $250 without prior approval, and supervisors to refund up to $10,000 over the phone. The $250 limit is based on an analysis of the average cost of handling and settling complaints and compensation claims.

The focus at FedEx is on making sure the customer's view is fully understood and responded to and taking personal ownership for resolution of issues.

FedEx will refund even when they have done everything right. Along with a refund, however, the customer will receive an explanation of how the process should work and the event will be logged for reference should it happen again with that customer.

Management Information (MI) is used twice weekly to track causes of problems and instigate remedial action.

The cardinal sin is for a representative to let a customer off the phone who is not satisfied. Reps will always ask the customer directly if they are satisfied.

With all complaints logged, if a customer calls back with a query or follow-up complaint on the same issue, this re-opened complaint counts double in complaints statistics and towards bonus payments. The aim is for 99 per cent first-call resolution.

Gestures of goodwill

Complaint handlers often get confused about what is compensation and what is a gesture of goodwill. As an organization you may decide to offer a customer a gesture of goodwill. Gestures of goodwill apply in situations where the company has not made an error, whereas compensation is when the company has.

For example, a customer may complain and on investigating their complaint you see that this is not justified as the company was not at fault. However, you can see that there has been some genuine misunderstanding between the customer and the company. In this circumstance, although the company is not in the wrong, you may decide to offer a gesture of goodwill. This again can be financial or a gift or token.

Applying redress fairly can be a big issue for many firms. Make sure you do not make judgements based on the value of the customer to the business before you decide what amount of redress to give. I find this unacceptable and certainly not fair on other customers who may be less profitable to the business. Irrespective of size or profitability, all customers should have the right to have their complaint handled fairly.

One way to ensure this is to develop a clear policy on redress and to provide training to complaint-handling staff in how to apply it. I will come back to this topic in later chapters. You also need to make sure that your complaint-quality-assurance process measures whether a fair outcome was arrived at for the customer and whether appropriate redress was applied.

For legal and regulatory purposes it is important to confirm what redress or remedial action you are taking both on the phone and in writing to the customer. Break down the component parts if you are applying various types of redress; for example, the bank gave me both a refund and compensation for their error.

Service guarantees

If your organization is confident about the quality of any aspect of your service, you may wish to consider offering a service guarantee. Service providers offer their customers guarantees that provide a refund or compensation if the service offered fails to meet certain conditions. This is popular with organizations ranging from pizza parlours to utility companies. When there is an up-front policy that offers clear compensation for when the commitment is not met, customers have an assured outcome and know in advance what to expect, so complaints are minimal.

Service guarantees can become a source of competitive advantage. For example, a pizza chain may guarantee that if it fails to deliver within a certain time the pizza is free. In Canada a major food retailer has a service guarantee policy around the accuracy of its checkout scanners. If the customer finds that the price at the checkout is higher than the price shown for the product on the shelf, the customer gets the product for free, up to a $10 limit. If the product is over this price, the customer gets a $10 discount. This service guarantee stimulates staff to ensure that the prices are accurate. It also sends a strong promise to customers that the store is honest.

There is some evidence that offering this type of guarantee builds consumer confidence and helps prevent complaints. For example, Whitbread Travel Inn, which was the market leader in budget hotels, launched their 100 per cent Good Night satisfaction guarantee (or your money back) across the brand in 2001. For the 18 months that the campaign ran, the organization saw a marked decrease in complaints.

Key learning points

- Customers who complain are looking for a speedy resolution to their complaint.
- Customers want their complaint to be taken seriously.
- They want to be treated with empathy and receive an apology.
- Only a small proportion of customers are actively seeking financial recompense as a result of a complaint.
- When applying redress, businesses should ensure that they treat customers fairly.
- If the organization has made an error and the customer's complaint is justified, reimbursement, refund or compensation may be appropriate. Compensation can be financial or non-financial.
- If the organization is not at fault but, for example, there has been a genuine misunderstanding, a gesture of goodwill may be appropriate.

Customer complaint-handling checklist

Here is a detailed checklist based on customer research around the best-practice behaviours that will help your organization to meet customer expectations when it comes to complaints.

Use the list to assess how well your business responds to customer complaints. Consider how your organization deals with complaints from a customer's perspective. Give your organization a rating out of 10 (where 1 = poor and 10 = excellent) for each aspect on this list.

When making a complaint, customers expect to:

Contact the organization easily by any method that they want. — Your score: ___

Have their complaint dealt with speedily and in the majority of cases have telephone contact from the organization. — Your score: ___

Deal with someone who shows understanding of the issue. — Your score: ___

Deal with a named contact who takes responsibility for their complaint and is empowered to make a decision about it. — Your score: ___

Deal with professional and polite members of staff. — Your score: ___

Be treated fairly as a person not a number. — Your score: ___

Have their complaint investigated fairly and thoroughly. — Your score: ___

Be told the truth and receive an apology if the organization is at fault. — Your score: ___

Receive a detailed response to all the issues raised. — Your score: ___

Have detailed reasons if the outcome of the complaint is not what they wanted. — Your score: ___

Deal with an organization that follows through on action and keeps its promises. — Your score: ___

Know that the organization has taken action to improve as a result of complaints. — Your score: ___

Customer-management strategy and its implementation

04

Managers have a key role to play in setting the climate and culture around complaint handling in their organizations.

In this chapter I outline the need for a clear organizational strategy in relation to complaints. I also look at some of the 'harder' elements that are needed for effective complaint management, such as a clearly communicated policy, customer-focused processes and procedures and an effective system for recording and tracking complaints.

I also look at the 'softer' elements of the strategy including recruitment and retention of complaint handlers and the issue of empowerment and measurement.

Setting a strategy for your complaint management

If you are intending to set up or work in a complaint-handling department, or if you already work in a complaint-handling or customer-service function, it is essential that you and others are clear what your organization's strategy is around complaint handling. What are you trying to achieve? For example, do you recognize complaint handling as a key customer retention activity and view it as an opportunity to learn and improve? Or is complaint management a cost to the organization that needs to be minimized?

If your organization operates in a regulated environment, you may also want to define your 'risk appetite' for complaints. In other words, do you want to be 100 per cent compliant with your industry regulations or are you prepared to accept lower standards? Have you considered the mitigating actions your business needs to take to lower the risk of non-compliance?

In many sectors where there are regulations about the way complaints are handled, there is a requirement for firms to appoint a senior manager who acts as a nominated official around complaints. They are also often legally responsible and can be personally fined if the organization is found to be non-compliant.

Link to organizational vision and values

Best-practice complaint-management strategies are aligned to what the organization is trying to achieve and to its values. So, for example, Walt Disney's company mission statement is 'to make people happy'. The company also has the following values:

- no cynicism;
- nurturing and promulgation of 'wholesome American values';
- creativity, dreams and imagination;
- fanatical attention to consistency and detail;
- preservation and control of the Disney 'magic'.

Disney recruits and trains people who want to make the guest experience magical. As part of every 'cast member's' (employee's) training, Disney makes it clear that it does not tolerate workers that are anything less than 'magical'. If customers complain about this, the chances are that the employee will be dismissed.

Organizational values will clearly differ from company to company but in essence they should encompass the bloodline of the organization. Here are some examples of companies with strong values.

Technology company Microsoft's values are integrity, honesty, openness, personal excellence, constructive self-criticism, continual self-improvement and mutual respect. The company states it is committed to its customers and partners and has a passion for technology. Its website goes on to say: 'We take on big challenges, and pride ourselves on seeing them through. We hold ourselves accountable to our customers, shareholders, partners, and employees by honouring our commitments, providing results, and striving for the highest quality.'

Telephone and internet banking service first direct is an example of an organization that has revolutionized the banking industry by its drive to provide a flexible service to the customer. It offers an attractive product and service to its customers at a competitive price. Its 24-hour service, 365 days a year, means it is constantly accessible to its customers both on the phone and via the internet.

First direct has succeeded by having a clear vision and set of values that focus on the customer. It recruits customer-focused employees who match its values. Its philosophy is that it can train skills but that new recruits need to come with a positive attitude. First direct is the most recommended of all UK banks and constantly receives the highest scores in terms of customer satisfaction.

Best practice organizations therefore link their complaint handling strategies to their values. However, Interestingly, there are organizations that appear not to want to help customers when it comes to complaints. A British television programme called *Airport* parodied airline staff that were inflexible and bound by procedure. Employees depicted on the programme appeared to guard the rest of the organization from customers who complained and adopted the approach of 'comply with our rules or don't use our service.'

Does consumers' search for low-cost, best-value products and services mean that they are prepared to accept poor customer service? I think not. However, many low-cost businesses have procedures that appear to benefit the organization, not the customer. There appears to be an avoidance of human interaction and/or inflexible processes aimed at making customers compliant to the organization's rules that leave the customer feeling helpless and frustrated.

Lily Allen, the celebrity I referred to earlier, tweeted that she had to pay £40 for low-cost airline Ryanair to print her boarding card at the airport as she had forgotten to print this herself. She had the piece of paper in her possession for seven minutes after it was printed before she had to give it back to the airline as she boarded the plane. The airline did not respond.

Hard and soft elements of a complaint-management strategy

Figure 4.1 illustrates how a complaint-management strategy should be the umbrella for both the task ('hard') and people ('soft') elements of complaint management and how measurement, learning and improvement complete the feedback loop. Excellent complaint management can only occur when all the elements in the circle are aligned.

Complaint-management policy and standards

Having an effective and transparent policy for the fair and prompt handling of complaints is essential for all businesses. This should be easily accessible to customers and publicized for all to see.

For example transport body TfL (Transport for London) has a policy that sets out how it deals with customers. This covers the following headings:

- easy to access;
- confidential;
- informative and simple;
- fair and effective;
- monitored and acted upon.

In the section 'Fair and effective', it says that where customer feedback relates to a problem, the organization will provide:

- an explanation;
- details of what actions will be taken (where relevant);
- an apology if it is due;
- a description of what we will do to prevent the same thing happening again (if possible);
- a refund of the fare paid or financial compensation if appropriate.

FIGURE 4.1 Complaint-management strategy loop

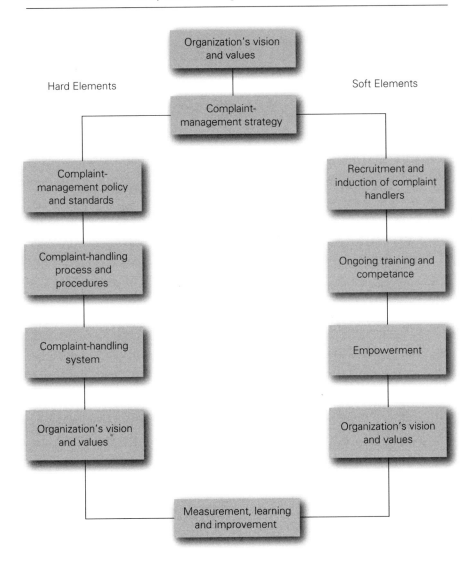

Customer-complaint policies should include information on how and where to complain, and the timescales for dealing with complaints. They should be written in a way that is easy for customers to understand and use. As discussed earlier, customers also want to be provided with a variety of communication channels through which to complain, for instance telephone, mail, face-to-face, fax and e-channels.

Customers must also be made aware of any rights to refer unresolved disputes to independent arbitrators or regulators.

It is important that this policy is accessible and understood by employees. Best practice is to make complaint management part of every employee's induction and, where relevant, annual training plan.

Internally, the complaints policy and standards need to cover methods, roles and responsibilities for:

- receiving and recording complaints;
- investigating and responding to complaints;
- complaint escalation procedures;
- how to comply with regulatory and legal guidance published by relevant regulators, advisers and dispute resolution bodies (eg industry ombudsmen);
- applying redress where appropriate;
- retention of complaint records;
- reporting complaints data.

The policy standards need to be reviewed on a regular basis to ensure that they are relevant and are being applied. Later I will talk about measuring the standards and closing the customer-feedback loop.

Complaint-handling processes and procedures

Your complaint-management policy should make clear to everyone the processes and procedures that you will use for handling complaints. There is much debate around whether it is better to have a centralized or decentralized approach to complaints. In other words, should members of staff be able to resolve a complaint at the first point of contact or should all complaints be handed off to a centralized, specialist team? Should you outsource your complaints?

There are pros and cons for each approach and a lot depends on the industry sector in which you operate. Retailer DSG brought its call centre back in-house and has seen greater effectiveness in the resolution of customer complaints as a result.

If you are or are going to operate a centralized system, it is essential to agree hand-off processes and timescales for passing on complaints and make sure that everyone is aware of these. Likewise it is useful to set service-level agreements, including timescales for information flow between different parts of the business that may be contacted by a centralized team investigating the complaint.

Whatever process you adopt, training is required to ensure that employees are clear about the steps and their roles and responsibilities.

In the financial services sector in the UK, for example, the regulator requires all firms to adopt by 2012 a 'one-stage' as opposed to a 'two-stage' operating model for responding to complaints. Under these new rules, a firm's first response to a customer about a complaint must be its final response. The Financial Services Authority (FSA) hopes that this change will encourage firms to resolve complaints fairly, right first time. It found that using a 'two-stage' process (where the response the organization issued to a complaint after the investigation was not final and could be changed) relied on a customer's persistence – or lack thereof – when pursuing a complaint. This it found was not fair to customers.

Complaint-handling system

Telecoms giant AT&T has a single complaint-management system to handle complaints from inception through to resolution. All staff dealing with complaints are required to connect to the Complaint Tracking System. This system provides:

- access to current and past customer data;
- daily statistics, and trend analysis that is compared to baseline from other organizations believed to be best-in-class;
- reporting mechanisms for passing complaint information to senior management, allowing them to keep abreast of the top customer issues, customer expectations and satisfaction levels.

As a result, AT&T believes it is better able to quickly identify how complaints are being dealt with and reward excellent service and behaviour exhibited by its staff.

Southwark Council is a three-star local authority that has been recognized for providing value-for-money services to its residents. It provides residents and local businesses with more than 200 services, from refuse collection to education and housing. Southwark welcomed complaints, compliments and queries from its users but did not have a central point of contact for its customers. Different services dealt with and held different complaint data; often this was duplicated and not shared across the organization. The council decided to set up one customer-service centre for all its services, with one common process for complaint management. It invested in a complaint-management system and provided training for customer-service staff. The solution allowed Southwark to increase the number of complaints resolved at the same time as reducing complaint resolution times. It also provided Southwark with valuable root-cause analysis information that has driven more efficient and effective practices across the authority.

Best-practice organizations ensure that they have effective complaint-management systems in place to facilitate the full and accurate recording of all complaints at the earliest opportunity. Automated systems can link with a business's existing databases or stand alone. Whatever the system you use, at a minimum it will need to enable you to record:

- customer details;
- where and when the complaint was received;
- who is dealing with the complaint;
- what the complaint is about, to allow thorough investigation, accurate root-cause analysis and improvement activity;
- details of all communications with the customer;
- progress updates on the current position and actions taken and/or planned;
- details of the investigation;
- details of the decision on the case (whether the complaint was upheld or not);
- remedial actions and redress if appropriate;
- follow up action;
- customer feedback;
- compliance with regulatory requirements.

And it will help you analyse data and trends.

My experience is that many systems are over-complicated or not accessible across the organization. This leads to a reluctance of employees to record complaints, and to the organization missing valuable insights.

Many complaint-management systems can now link directly to web-based customer feedback options. Organizations in the public service sector, for example, are increasingly providing online feedback options to allow customers to log their own complaints. At Stoke-on-Trent City Council, customers can record their dissatisfaction on the council's website. This is automatically linked to the organization's complaint-management system. The council has seen a doubling in the number of complaints that it handles over the past five years. However, it sees this as a good thing as the feedback it has received has allowed it to identify and prioritize key areas for improvement such as education and road services.

The people side

The right-hand side of the complaint-management strategy circle involves people. Employees who handle complaints must be competent to recognize and deal with them effectively.

Recruitment

Hiring the right kind of people as complaint handlers is key to delivering excellent service. It can also dramatically reduce attrition rates. One contact centre I worked with reduced its attrition from 76 per cent to 13 per cent annually by profiling its best agents and then using psychometric testing to assess how well candidates matched the ideal profile. The cost of psychometric testing was more than offset by the money saved in not re-recruiting and training new staff. Another customer-relations department greatly improved its recruitment of complaint handlers by designing a robust assessment of potential agents. This involved both a telephone assessment around a complaint as well as a letter-writing assessment and an assessment of the candidates' awareness of the regulatory environment.

There is a growing use of assessment centres to help identify the best candidates. Cambridgeshire County Council uses a one-day session at an assessment centre to identify potential customer-service recruits. This includes telephony trials, team exercises and observation exercises. Candidates who pass the assessment are called for an in-depth interview. This process has helped the council identify people who have a real desire to help the customer and who demonstrate empathy.

When recruiting, I recommend that you are honest with potential candidates about your working environment. If you are looking for 'foot soldiers', do not recruit 'cavalry'. Much work in a customer-service environment can be routine and process-driven. It is no use recruiting people who look for variety and want to avoid repetition if this is the case.

Insurance company Aviva profiled its best performing agents and developed a set of assessment criteria that included behaviours such as listening skills, empathy, flexibility and confidence. It devised a recruitment advertising pro-gramme that reflected these key qualities. When candidates applied for the job, they were assessed against these criteria. They also sat in the call centre and shadowed an agent so that they got a good idea of what the job actually entailed. The quality of people that applied for the post was higher using this method than other recruitment campaigns, although fewer people applied. As a result, retention increased by 50 per cent and customer satisfaction by 15 per cent.

Induction

Successful organizations recognize how powerful induction is in shaping people's attitude to the business and to the customer. It is said that up to 20 per cent of new recruits do not turn up to a job because they are too nervous.

Supermarket chain Waitrose, part of the John Lewis Partnership, has actively taken steps to make new recruits feel special prior to and as they join the company. They issue a special welcome pack including a DVD before people join and hold thorough inductions, including product tast-ings. Other companies have used Facebook to show case studies and provide information to new recruits before they start with the company. Wine merchant Laithwaites sends four or five people every couple of weeks to work in its wine-making site in Bordeaux. They answer the phones and make calls as if they were in the UK, but get to visit wine producers as well.

Dignity Caring Funeral Services is the UK's leading funeral plan provider. It also offers funeral services through its chain of funeral parlours. Its recruitment process places emphasis on finding people who are caring and sympathetic. Recognized as a top performer in its sector, it provides new starters in its client-service centre with a five-week induction. This includes a visit to a funeral home. Empathy is very important in the role and is a key part of the induction training programme.

Once in the job, if people do leave the complaints team, it is important to find out why. Best-practice organizations take time to find out why the job did not meet their expectations and what changes the leaver would recommend to encourage other people to stay.

Training and competence

Complaint handlers have an essential role in reassuring customers, dealing with their complaints quickly and fairly, and making sure they arrive at a fair outcome and prevent any mistakes happening again.

Make sure that everyone in your complaint-handling team receives training. John Lewis has trained all 30,000 of its staff to ensure consistency in customer service. Training includes product knowledge, and customer-service and selling skills. All partners, including all members of its three contact centre teams, are trained at different levels, defined by how much product knowledge they are given.

In the United States, financial services provider Citigroup put in place a programme to create a positive customer experience and perception. It encouraged customer feedback directly through the branch, telephone, in writing or social media channels. Citigroup responds to customers through their preferred channel. Irrespective of the channel the customer chooses, the customer-service representatives are able to deliver a consistent message. This is reinforced by an intensive training programme both around behaviours and skills and around systems. Customer complaints received through any channel are entered into a central complaint-management system and then sent to the appropriate department for resolution.

In order to ensure that employees are competent to deal with complaints effectively (and that they remain competent), it is useful to develop a complaint-handling competency framework. This can set out the level of business knowledge required as well as the skills and behaviours identified for each role.

We worked with one centralized complaints team to develop four levels of competency for complaint handlers; these are incremental (eg to achieve Level 2 on the competency ladder, you had to first demonstrate competency at Level 1) and apply to all roles in the team. An overview of the four levels is:

Level 1.   Is able to deal with routine complaints on the phone and in writing.

Level 2.   Is able to deal with more complex complaints.

Level 3.   Is able to quality-assure and coach others around effective complaint handling.

Level 4.   Is able to manage, lead and supervise the complaint-handling team.

There were corresponding knowledge, skills and behaviour requirements that provided clear guidance to employees on what level of complaint-handling competence their role required and how to achieve it.

By developing a competency framework, the function was better able to align its training and development activities to individual needs. In the next chapter I talk in more depth about the skills and behaviours needed by complaint-handling staff. Needless to say, to attain competency and remain competent, individuals need ongoing training and development. I am also a great advocate of coaching. For one organization we designed and delivered five days of specialist complaint-handling training. We also trained managers and team leaders in coaching skills. Once the training was completed, managers and team leaders coached the team on a one-to-one basis, using the coaching framework I describe in the next chapter. As a result, the time complaint handlers took to attain the next level of competency was cut by half.

The benefit of having a training and competency framework is that complaint handlers can see a career path and talent can be developed. During one-to-one performance reviews, employees can discuss evidence of how they have demonstrated key knowledge, skills and behaviours, as can line managers through quality assurance, observations and case reviews. The staff member can also evidence development activity and agree with their manager a development plan where competence has not been achieved.

Empowerment

It can be very annoying when you make a complaint as a customer and no one will take ownership or responsibility for the problem. Equally annoying is when no one has any authority to resolve a complaint. Lack of empowerment can be very frustrating to the customer.

One of my colleagues ordered a desk online and paid for it to be delivered to her student son. The desk got lost in transit. When my colleague called to complain, no one was empowered to make a decision about what to do. She was told that she had to wait seven days for the desk to potentially turn up. After this time, the complaint was passed to a centralized team who processed the complaint online without contacting the customer. They offered £50 standard compensation, which did not reflect the cost of the desk, the inconvenience or distress the situation had caused. When my colleague did eventually manage to speak to a person in the complaints team about the situation, she was told that he had been told by his supervisor that he had no authority to act otherwise, otherwise he would lose marks for quality. The supervisor had told him the customer could 'take it or leave it'.

The majority of complaint-handling teams are situated in contact centres. Over the past decade there has been a phenomenal growth in the number of centres that provide service and advice to customers. However, jobs in call centres continue to be designed with low levels of autonomy. An international study, The Global Call Centre Project, surveyed almost 2,500 centres in 17 countries. It found that the vast majority of contact centre agents have their performance continually monitored and have low levels of discretion around how they deal with customers, have to follow scripts, take their breaks at set times. It also identified that typical levels of turnover in call centres where there was more autonomy and better-quality jobs were 9 per cent, whereas turnover is 36 per cent per annum for low-quality jobs.

Psychologists explain that when people experience a loss of control, they retaliate the only way they can: either physically by going sick or mentally by not caring and delivering poor levels of customer service. There is a direct link between loss of autonomy and low motivation and depression.

Many businesses, such as breakdown provider RAC, are moving away from a scripted customer-service environment. Financial services organization ING Direct has also stopped asking its customer-service agents to use scripts in their interactions with customers. It implemented an empowerment training programme with the aim of putting the customer at the heart of the interaction. This was a leap of faith for a company in a regulated environment, and has resulted in a more positive experience for the customers and the agents, who can personalize and develop their own style on the call.

In terms of complaint handling, customer research demonstrates that customers prefer their complaint to be dealt with by people who can make a decision there and then. This means empowering your complaint handlers to do what is best for the customer. This involves providing guidance to team members in terms of best practice, whilst at the same time allowing them the discretion to do what is right for the customer, taking the individual circumstances of the complaint into account.

In Ireland, supermarket chain Superquinn encourages its managers to visit customers in their home if they have had a problem in the store. They are given the widest possible scope to take responsibility for a complaint and are able to settle an issue using their discretion.

At luxury hotel group Ritz Carlton, staff are empowered at every level to spend up to $2,000 to satisfy a guest and resolve a complaint. To deal with complaints as close to the front line as possible, staff at Ritz Carlton hotels have clearly defined levels of authority to decide action. There are clear procedures in place to ensure that the employee who first hears about the problem subsequently owns the problem and is responsible for finding a solution or escalating.

To help staff understand the customer more fully and therefore take informed action, all Ritz Carlton employees are trained to read customer reactions and detect their likes and dislikes. These preferences are entered into a guest history profile database that provides information about the preferences of 250,000 guests. This enables staff to understand complainants and what they expect, and therefore to take actions to resolve the complaint.

A company that has also encouraged greater empowerment is American Express, one of the leading payment, travel and card-issuing companies. Its vision is 'to become the world's most respected service brand'. Service has been a part of its brand heritage, but some five years ago the business appeared to be focusing too much on managing service as a cost centre. In an increasingly competitive industry, American Express leadership believed that it needed to redefine its approach to service in order to gain competitive advantage.

Over the years the company had become increasingly reliant on call centre interaction as the principal means of establishing a relationship with its customers. It found it had moved to a highly data-driven approach to customer service and believed it was losing the human element in its interactions with customers. Customer satisfaction scores were not improving and turnover at the company's principal contact centre in Phoenix was running at a high level. The conversations agents were having with customers were highly scripted. Agents had low levels of autonomy and discretion in their work. In addition the measures used to performance-manage call centre staff focused on the number of transactions per agent per day. Customer-service staff were monitored on a variety of elements, such as saying the customer's name three times during a call.

In a bold move to increase the level of customer satisfaction and retention, American Express developed a new strategy called 'Relationship Care'. This placed great emphasis on customer service not as a back-office cost centre but as central to the business's success. The focus was shifted from seeing the customer's call as a transaction to seeing it as an opportunity to build a great relationship.

The changes made to encourage greater empowerment included:

- Scripts were discarded and staff were trained to engage with the customer and create an emotional connection.
- There was greater autonomy in decision making.
- Customer-care professionals (CCPs) are now measured by their customers, each CCP receiving direct feedback on a proportion of their calls from customers.
- The firm changed the remuneration structure, making a proportion of incentive pay linked to whether customers would 'recommend a friend'.

- It changed its recruitment policy and upgraded its training. It provided training to CCPs in relationship-management skills.

- It set up a robust talent-management progression and enhanced career progression opportunities – four levels of progression instead of one.

- It focused on achieving a better work–life balance and offered flexible scheduling. The firm offers an on-site health clinic, exercise classes and workshops in financial planning.

- It introduced a new IT system to help CCPs personalize discussions with customers and recognize the products they were using and identify opportunities for them to adopt others.

- It made symbolic changes, such as changing the agents' title from 'customer care representative' to 'customer care professional' and giving CCPs business cards for the first time.

As a result of the Relationship Care programme, customer satisfaction scores have increased. American Express has earned top ranking among credit card providers from its customers for the past three years. Attrition has fallen and so have training costs as there is now a more stable workforce.

Measurement

Be careful what you measure. I have worked with a number of customer-service departments where what was measured drove the wrong behaviour. For example, one customer-relations function set targets around the number of complaints closed-off each day. Agents received a bonus if they reached these targets. As a result, agents 'cherry-picked' the complaints they wanted. They worked on ones that were easiest to handle. Staff avoided complex complaints as they took longer to resolve and prevented them from reaching their targets. The same applied in another company where agents were incentivized on the number of calls made to customers to resolve complaints. The organization found that agents deliberately transferred long or complex complaint calls or even hung up because they did not want to miss their targets.

Many customer-relations departments are now obtaining personalized feedback from customers about each agent. They are using this as their principal metric rather than the time agents spend on the phone or how quickly they resolve complaints.

At telecoms retailer Carphone Warehouse, staff are encouraged to take responsibility for resolving complaints. Each store has a 'net promoter score' that measures customer satisfaction and loyalty. Individuals are incentivized on achieving team and customer metrics, not sales.

Make sure that your quality measures, therefore, are driving the right behaviours and that your management and quality-assurance team are fully aligned to your customer-management strategy; avoid giving your customers the type of experience that happened to my colleague whose desk was lost in transit.

Consider creating a recognition scheme for customer-service staff and complaint handlers. Being praised and thanked for a job well done or for delivering excellent service is a powerful motivator.

Logistics company FedEx has a strong philosophy around putting people first. It knows that as a result employees will provide superior service to customers, resulting in greater profitability. FedEx actively rewards and recognizes customer service in two principal ways: the Golden Falcon Award, which is awarded when customers tell the company about people who exceed their expectations with 'above and beyond' service; and a reward called Bravo Zulu, where managers are able to reward people on the spot with a cash bonus of $100.

Also in the United States, Continental Airlines recognizes and rewards efforts staff take to reduce complaints. It had experienced a large increase in complaints because of poor punctuality that resulted in increased costs, delays, stranded passengers and lost business. To improve the situation, the CEO promised that for each month Continental was in the top half of the punctuality league, every employee would share equally in half of the $6 million savings Continental could make from increased punctuality. By the second month, Continental had moved from bottom to top of the punctuality league table and premium-fare business passengers started returning.

Learning and improvement

Both the hard and soft sides of the complaint-management circle are closed by learning and making improvements as a result of complaints.

Ultimately, an effective complaint-management strategy should allow you to identify and remedy causes of complaints, and so to improve products, systems, policies, processes and service. Where appropriate, action should also be taken on behalf of customers affected by a complaint even if they have not complained.

Key learning points

- Develop or review your complaint-management strategy.

- Ensure that both the 'hard' and the 'soft' elements are effective and aligned in order to ensure a customer focus.

Seven Ss assessment

Management consultancy McKinsey has developed a method for analysing organizations and their effectiveness. It looks at the seven key elements that make organizations successful: strategy, structure, systems, style, skills, staff and shared values. It can be applied to complaint handling and is a useful framework that summarizes the lessons of this chapter.

FIGURE 4.2 The seven Ss

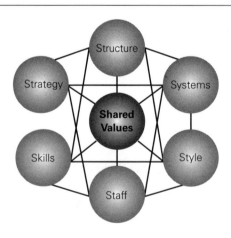

Rate your organization against the seven Ss in relation to complaint management on a scale of 1 (low) to 10 (high):

We have a clear **strategy** in place for complaint management that encourages timely and fair resolution and learning from complaints.

1___ 2___ 3___ 4___ 5___ 6___ 7___ 8___ 9___ 10

We have **structured** our complaint-handling teams in a way that encourages ownership and cooperation.

1___ 2___ 3___ 4___ 5___ 6___ 7___ 8___ 9___ 10

Our complaint **systems** and processes help engender fair, timely resolution.

1___ 2___ 3___ 4___ 5___ 6___ 7___ 8___ 9___ 10

Our **staff** are empowered to resolve complaints effectively.

1___ 2___ 3___ 4___ 5___ 6___ 7___ 8___ 9___ 10

Team members have the **skills**, knowledge and behaviour training to ensure they are competent and remain competent.

1___ 2___ 3___ 4___ 5___ 6___ 7___ 8___ 9___ 10

Our organization has a set of **shared values** that encourage a customer focus.

1___ 2___ 3___ 4___ 5___ 6___ 7___ 8___ 9___ 10

Leaders' and managers' **style** is a role model of customer focus.

1___ 2___ 3___ 4___ 5___ 6___ 7___ 8___ 9___ 10

Communication styles and emotional intelligence

05

Before looking at the skills and behaviours needed to deal with complaints well, it is useful to understand the approaches that complainants take in communicating their dissatisfaction and how emotional intelligence can help effective complaint handling. This chapter addresses these two topics.

Ways people choose to complain

The complaints scenario presents an opportunity to forge a stronger relationship with the customer when complaint handlers show a real desire to resolve the customer's issues. It also presents an opportunity to demonstrate real empathy and competence.

When there was a major oil spill in the Gulf of Mexico in 2010, the oil firm BP was criticized in the United States for its crisis-management performance. Tony Hayward, BP's then CEO, was attacked for his lack of empathy and initial silence about the situation. His communication style in the crisis was attacked by the American general public.

Although complaints are not an oil spill, metaphorically they can provoke the same degree of emotional response and long-term damage if the service provider does not respond appropriately.

As we have seen earlier, when something goes wrong for the customer, he or she incurs an emotional as well as an economic cost. When customers are annoyed, frustrated or angry, they can choose one of four styles to voice their complaint. They can address the issue in a manner that is:

- assertive;
- passive;
- aggressive;
- passive-aggressive.

Figure 5.1 gives a summary of the four communication styles.

FIGURE 5.1   The four communication styles

Assertive behaviour	Displaying confidence in communicating yet at the same time considering the views of others. This behaviour allows individuals to communicate their thoughts and feelings in a respectful way.
Passive behaviour	Displaying little or no concern for their own needs or feelings and more concerned with the views and feelings of others. This behaviour breeds low self-esteem and withdrawal.
Aggressive behaviour	Displaying a lot of confidence in communication but giving little consideration to needs, thoughts or feelings of others. This behaviour may be described as domineering or self-centred.
Passive-aggressive behaviour	Displaying little confidence in communication or consideration of others. Passive-aggressives find subtle ways to convey their thoughts or feelings. This behaviour is not direct and is often perceived as manipulative.

The person receiving the complaint can quickly tell the communication style that customers are using from their tone of voice, the words they use and the customer's body language if the complaint is made face to face.

Assertiveness is a learned behaviour and can be built with practice and over time. The issue for complaint handlers is that in difficult situations customers often revert to instinctive behaviours, leading to aggressive, passive-aggressive or passive communication. This sometimes makes the situation very difficult to handle from a customer-service perspective.

Passive behaviour is characterized by shying away from conflict, giving in or changing one's mind without valid reason and putting oneself down. Typically, passive customers may not even bother to complain and may be part of the silent majority who simply decide it is not worth it. If they do complain, they are softly spoken, avert their gaze and tend to make light of their complaint, saying things like: 'It's just a little thing,' 'I'm sorry to bother you,' 'I don't mean to be a nuisance.'

Customers who adopt an aggressive style are likely to dominate the conversation, potentially ignoring the service provider's views and not listening. In extreme cases they may use bad language, shout and swear. Their manner can be accusatory and they often raise their voice. Essentially these customers relish a fight.

People who complain and adopt a passive-aggressive stance tend to blame the organization, and can be cynical and discourteous. They use sarcasm to indicate they are not happy, or give out verbal and non-verbal cues such as tutting and raising their eyes to the ceiling.

When people deal with an assertive customer, there is a two-way dialogue. The conversation is calm and constructive and the outcome tends to be win–win.

How complaint handlers choose to respond

Behaviour is a choice. Those people who deal with complaints and fight back when the customer is aggressive, or meet sarcasm with sarcasm when dealing with passive-aggressive customers, do not help resolve the situation.

Remember to remain assertive in your response. Practise techniques such as thinking positive thoughts or taking a deep breath to help you to keep calm and not rise to the bait. Pause before you say anything so you can collect your thoughts. If you are standing facing the customer, move slightly to one side so that you are not standing directly opposite. This is less confrontational.

In dealing with customer complaints, the customer-service professional needs to demonstrate two key attributes: consideration for others and confidence in communicating; in other words, an assertive communication style.

Consideration can be described as the ability to show empathy for the customer's point of view, and it can also be thought of as the ability to put on the shoes of another person – to step into their world and see the situation from their perspective. At the same time, the customer-service representative needs to present him/herself and the organization's view with confidence. Assertiveness therefore is the best approach that an agent should take, no matter what style of communication the customer is using, either face to face, on the phone or in writing.

Emotional intelligence

As customers we recognize good or bad service as soon as we receive it. As service providers, however, we are frequently in danger of failing to recognize the sensitivities and needs of the customer, particularly when they complain.

In my experience the best customer-service professionals show high levels of emotional quotient (EQ), otherwise known as emotional intelligence. In Figure 5.2, this relates to 'consideration for others', the ability to put yourself in the customer's shoes and to see things from their perspective.

Why EQ is important in delivering excellent service

The most 'efficient' organizations are not always the most customer friendly. Research by Daniel Goleman, author of *Working with Emotional Intelligence*, indicates that when it comes to lasting relationships it is more often our personality and the way we relate to customers rather than specialist technical skills that count with others. Supermarket chain ASDA has grown increasingly successful by projecting a cheerful and responsive approach to each customer. At online bank first direct, customer response staff are trained to respond individually to the mood and needs of each customer.

FIGURE 5.2 Confidence and consideration for others

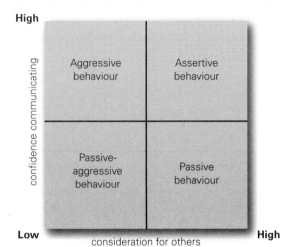

Service providers who are emotionally intelligent are those who have high awareness of:

- themselves and the range and depth of their feelings – sad, happy, depressed;
- other people and their feelings, and what signals such feelings give off;
- the impact they have on others;
- the impact other people have on them.

They are able to use this knowledge to manage the way they deal with other people and to change the impact that others have on them or that they have on the customer.

All complaint handlers know that handling multiple customer complaints each day puts them under pressure. It is very easy to take things personally, to become frustrated and stressed. Service providers with high emotional intelligence recognize their emotional temperatures and are able to control their effects. They take steps to proactively manage their stress levels and the way stress comes out.

When handling customer complaints, particularly difficult ones, the ability to empathize with the customer is a key skill. Service providers with high levels of EQ create rapport with customers by speaking the customers' own language, showing an interest and relating to what the customers are feeling. In this way they form better relationships with customers that lead to more effective results and are able to defuse many difficult situations.

The reality: few customer-service organizations have high EQ

If a well-developed ability to empathize with the customer is clearly so important, why is it not universal in service organizations? What stops EQ being present throughout the organization? Here are some common reasons for poorly developed EQ:

Many managers are 'people insensitive'

Managers often reach positions of authority through their technical ability and their capacity to look dispassionately at facts and present information logically. The Myers-Briggs Type Indicator©* measures this as a preference for 'Decision making through thinking'. Research suggests that more managers are higher on this scale than 'Feeling', which is a preference for actively paying attention to others. A study of the relative ineffectiveness of IT managers when they were serving their internal clients observed: 'One of the more noticeable aspects is how many of them find it hard to get in touch with their feelings.' Such managers pay more attention to:

- facts rather than emotions;
- logic rather than sensitivities.

This approach affects the ability to listen more to customers and colleagues and to create and maintain rapport.

* Myers-Briggs Type Indicator is a registered trademark of Oxford Psychologist Press.

Many suffer from overload and stress

In an era of downsizing and the drive for 'more with less', employees feel increasingly under pressure as layers of the hierarchy have been removed. Fear can lead them to take on a 'siege mentality', afraid to delegate and closed to the views or feelings of others for fear there will be personal criticism, or that openness may lead to even more work for the individual involved.

There is a deluge of information

As information availability has increased, so has the difficulty for managers and organizations of handling the data. This has led to the situation where warning signs of poor quality or customer dissatisfaction go unheeded.

Interfaces have multiplied

The growth of outsourcing, alliances and global networks has led to more possibilities for confusion and distortion. Cultural differences and barriers can restrict the ability to understand and be understood.

Managers' fear of letting go

Many managers are reluctant to empower and are overly concerned to keep control. This leads to lack of trust, which others quickly pick up on. Management textbooks report the death of the autocrat and controller – we have seen plenty around the organizations we visit!

Poor role models

In view of what we have said so far, it is not surprising that senior managers often display negative and insensitive behaviours. In turn their managers and staff pick up the signals and behave in a similar way, and so the cycle repeats itself. For years one organization we worked with instilled a 'do as you're told' mentality. Latterly, it has been seeking new ideas and its top management are puzzled why there are so few who challenge the status quo. Old habits are hard to change. At a course dinner, the company's director harangued the managers for lack of challenge, whilst they all sat quietly, fearful of the consequences of speaking out on their careers.

Shielding of impact

We become shielded from the consequences of our actions. Employees of large organizations frequently do not personally feel the impact of their decisions. E-mail and voice mail have heightened this cocooning impact, which can lead to an approach of 'it wasn't my fault'.

How to increase your own EQ and that of your team

Unlike intelligence quotient (IQ), emotional intelligence is not static. It peaks in people's 50s and there is an equal distribution amongst both men and women. There are many approaches you can use to increase your own EQ and that of others who handle complaints and who work in customer-service environments. Here is a selection of methods:

- Find ways during recruitment to check out the level of candidates' EQ. For example, ask for detailed examples of how they handled difficult complaints. Watch for responses that indicate empathy and concern for the customer. Use an EQ diagnostic as an assessment tool.

- Encourage older workers in your complaint-handling department. You will often find they have higher levels of emotional intelligence.

- Mystery-shop your service: make a complaint to your organization. Ask your team to experience the service they provide from a customer's perspective and to identify the feelings this experience generates.

- Mystery-shop your competitors and encourage your team to do the same, noting how the needs of customers were met.

- Encourage your team to bring in examples of best practice in customer service, especially those that display EQ.

- Feed back comments from customers. As suggested in the previous chapter, use customer research to identify how each service provider is performing.

- Monitor performance and provide ongoing coaching. Focus on 'how' the service providers relate to the customer as well as on their knowledge or skills.

- Provide training in the skills needed in handling difficult customer situations. Put particular emphasis on showing genuine empathy to customers when they complain. Studies show that complaining customers will not listen until you show that you truly understand their situation.

- Engender a 'can-do' attitude in your team by empowering them to make decisions to help the customer.

- Coach your team in the use of rapport-building techniques such as recognizing customer moods and adapting service style to match, use of mirroring verbal and non-verbal cues (where appropriate), and showing a genuine interest in the customer.

- Talk with your team about how to deal with very difficult customer issues. Pass on this information to other parts of the organization so that steps can be taken to avoid similar complaints.

- Give feedback to your team on how they are performing – motivational feedback will develop their level of confidence and formative feedback will help them to improve. Be prepared to listen to feedback on your own performance.

- As part of your regular team meetings, talk about what causes your team stress. Take steps to overcome causes of stress. Provide training to your team in stress management.

- Make time to find out the expectations of colleagues and other groups. Encourage an internal customer approach to handling their expectations.

- Act as a role model for your team. Take time with them and give time to customers. Acknowledge what individuals in your team are feeling and offer them help and support.

Key learning points

- Many customers who complain react in a 'fight or flight' mode and can be aggressive, passive-aggressive or passive in their communication style.

- The best approach a complaint handler can take is to remain assertive, irrespective of the communication style the customer adopts.

- Effective complaint handlers show high levels of emotional intelligence. This is an aspect that should be encouraged and can be developed.

Assess your own EQ

Look at the following statements. Score each according to the extent to which you agree with it, where:

- Agree strongly: Score 5.
- Agree to some extent: Score 4.
- Neither agree or disagree: Score 3.
- Disagree somewhat: Score 2.
- Disagree strongly: Score 1.

Self-awareness	**Score**
1. I am aware of situations that cause me to think negatively.	
2. I recognize the emotions I feel when dealing with customers' complaints.	
3. I recognize what influences my way of thinking.	
4. I know when I am angry or sad.	
5. I know when I feel motivated and when I do not.	
6. I am confident in who I am.	
Total score: Self-awareness	

Awareness of own impact on others	**Score**
7. I know when I am not handling a customer situation well.	
8. I am aware of how my mood affects others around me.	
9. I have an accurate assessment of myself.	
10. I have received feedback from customers on the impact of my behaviours.	
11. I am aware when I make other people feel good about themselves.	
12. I know when my message is not clear to the customer.	
Total score: Awareness of own impact on others	

Awareness of others' emotions	**Score**
13. I can identify customers' emotion from their tone of voice.	
14. I am aware when customers are upset.	
15. I am able to put myself in the customers' shoes and acknowledge their feelings.	
16. I know when someone is not being sincere.	
17. I can understand when and why customers get angry.	
18. I notice when others say things that are inconsistent with what they appear to be feeling.	
Total score: Awareness of others' emotions	

Awareness of the impact of others' emotions on self   Score

19. I know which phrases customers use that upset me.

20. I am aware when customers are trying to manipulate me.

21. I know which types of customers I sympathize with more than others.

22. I know when someone is trying to get me to agree with them.

23. I recognize when customers make me angry.

24. I am aware when customers make me feel patronized.

Total score: Awareness of the impact of others' emotions on self

Ability to manage self   Score

25. I know how to control my emotions when customers get angry.

26. I am able to say 'no' to the customer without feeling guilty.

27. I am diplomatic.

28. I express what I am feeling in an appropriate manner.

29. I rarely take customer comments personally.

30. I can change my approach with a customer if my first attempt is not successful.

Total score: Ability to manage self

Analysing your scores

Look at the scores for each of the five sections above:

1 Self-awareness.

2 Awareness of own impact on others.

3 Awareness of others' emotions.

4 Awareness of the impact of others' emotions on self.

5 Ability to manage self.

You need to score over 24 out of 30 in all five sections if you are to be considered competent in creating and maintaining effective relationships with customers who complain. Look at the areas where you have low scores and consider the actions you can take to increase them.

The skills and behaviours needed for dealing effectively with complaints

06

This is a practical chapter. In it I build on the need to be assertive and demonstrate emotional intelligence when dealing with complaints. I set out the skills and behaviours needed for effective complaint management face to face and on the telephone. I also provide guidelines for handling written complaints.

To make this section come alive, I am going to relate the skills and behaviours of excellent complaint handlers to a customer complaint scenario.

Imagine you received this complaint on the phone

You left me in the lurch over the whole weekend. It was my daughter's wedding day on Saturday. I called you first thing on Friday morning when I noticed my drains were blocked and your contact centre promised faithfully someone would arrive that afternoon. I waited in until 5 pm, then I had to go to the airport. I had four family members staying plus two guests who had flown all the way from Australia. We had no toilet facilities all weekend. It was so embarrassing. I had to ask my neighbours if we could use their loo.

Not a good situation to be in, whatever the circumstances but particularly so at such an important time in one's life. So how do you respond to this complaint? I advocate a six-step process that will help you deal assertively and empathetically with any complaint.

Listen first

The temptation when you receive a call such as the one above is to immediately start taking details from the customer in an attempt to put the situation right. However, by focusing first on the facts of the situation, you are in danger of lacking emotional intelligence and not recognizing the emotional impact of the situation on the customer.

Most customers who complain use this as an opportunity to be heard. They want to explain their version of events and have the opportunity to vent their emotion. Yet most people do not listen at an emotional level. Or they listen for a few seconds, then interrupt. They do not hear the customer out. If the customer is angry, this can have the effect of making them angrier still.

In everyday listening we listen mostly to the words. The focus is on what the other person said and what you say in return. Mostly we hear the words and then disconnect from the conversation while we process internally what we have heard. We start thinking about what we'll say next. We listen at a superficial level as we evaluate and judge what the other person is saying.

In order to handle a complaint empathetically and assertively we need to listen at a deeper level. Only if we do this can we investigate the issues objectively and thoroughly and arrive at a fair outcome.

This means avoiding judgemental listening, where we listen to the customer at a superficial level and really are listening much more to our own thoughts and what we are going to say next. For example, you may be listening to the customer but thinking at the same time about how long he or she is taking to explain, that you have heard the same things many times before, that you have only 10 minutes till you need to go to a meeting so you need to wrap this up quickly.

The next level of listening is often called active or focused listening. If you are face to face and you are actively listening, people will see this in your and the customer's posture: both of you will be leaning forward, nodding, making eye contact. You pay a great deal of attention to what the customer is saying and don't pay much attention to the outside world. You listen to the customer's words, expressions, emotions: what that person is saying and how he or she says it.

This level of listening is about seeking to understand the customer's issues and concerns and acknowledging these. At this level the listeners' own internal chatter disappears and they no longer listen to their own thoughts or consider what they are going to say next. They follow the customer's lead, actively listen, check and acknowledge the customer. When you actively listen you use phrases with the customer such as:

- 'So what you're saying is...'
- 'To summarize, the key issues are...'
- 'Can I check my understanding...'
- 'So am I right in saying...'
- 'So what you're telling me is...'
- 'Have I understood you correctly, you're saying...'

There is also a deeper level of listening than active and focused listening. This is called intuitive listening. The complaint handler taps into his or her six senses and notices the customer's emotions – are they upset or calm about the situation? Is their energy sparking or flat? Are they cool and detached about the complaint or tightly controlled?

This is often described as tuning in to radio waves; emotions are entirely invisible but we trust they exist just as we hear music coming from the radio. Intuitive listening is about using one's emotional intelligence to tune in to the customer's situation and to understand what they are feeling and maybe even what they are not saying.

Typical phrases at this level of listening are:

- 'It seems as though...'
- 'It sounds like...'
- 'I can hear from your voice that...'
- 'I notice that you seem...'
- 'It sounds as though...'

In the customer complaint situation I described at the start of the chapter, if judgemental listening is all about you listening to yourself and active listening is focusing on the facts, intuitive listening is about what you are hearing in terms of the emotional impact on the customer. By truly listening and 'tuning in' to the customer's feeling you can show true empathy, which is the next step in the process.

Empathize and apologize

The first step to take in dealing with a complaint is to say sorry to the customer: that they have been inconvenienced, that they have had to complain, that they are frustrated. It does not matter at this stage whether or not the complaint arose because of something your company did wrong. 'Sorry' is a powerful word and customer-service professionals should not be afraid to say it. And to empathize with the customer.

Empathy involves identifying the customer's feelings and emotion and is a powerful rapport-building technique. This means acknowledging immediately what the customer is feeling. It is important to identify with the specific feeling. For example, in the situation we described earlier:

'I'm truly sorry to hear that. I do understand how disappointing and embarrassing the situation was on your daughter's big day...'

Be careful to make sure that the tone you use with the customer is sincere. Listen intuitively to pick up the underlying emotion the customer is feeling and acknowledge this. It is much more individual and personal than saying 'I understand how you feel,' which can sound patronizing and to which the customer is likely to answer: 'No you don't.'

Ask questions

It is only after you have said sorry and empathized that I recommend you focus on the facts. If you have not acknowledged the emotion of the situation first, the facts can be clouded by this.

The temptation when asking questions is to use closed questions that get a 'yes' or 'no' answer. In fact scientists say that our brain is wired to ask more closed questions than open ones. An open question allows you to receive more information than a closed one. Open questions start with: What, Where, Why, How, When, Who. It is better to ask open questions initially when trying to find out what happened from the customer. Open questions are useful to establish all the facts and allow customers to express their views. By asking open questions you build rapport and show you are interested in the customer's point of view.

'Tell me about', 'Explain' and 'Describe' are also useful in finding out the issues from the customer's perspective; for example 'So that I can help resolve the issue, please tell me what happened.'

So in this stage of the conversation with the customer, avoid using too many closed questions that produce a 'yes' or 'no' answer as this does not allow customers to express their thoughts and feelings on the issues. Avoid using leading questions such as 'You don't want me to write to you, do you?' This does not allow customers to express what they truly want.

You may need to explain why you are asking the question, so as to reassure the customer or to justify why you need the information. For example, 'So I can resolve this as quickly as possible, please tell me...'

Probing questions allow you to funnel down to gain further information; for example 'You said you had received a letter from us, what was the date on the letter?' If you need more detail from a customer, use words such as 'precisely', 'specifically', 'exactly' to get more information; for example 'I can see that must have been frustrating; what *precisely* happened?'

Asking for exact details is a useful technique when someone is in an emotional state. It is difficult to be angry when you have to be specific and precise.

Once you have the information that you need and you want the conversation to move forward, or when someone is being too detailed, ask the customer what the next steps would be for them. This is a particularly useful technique if you reach a stalemate with a customer. It also helps you to find out exactly what it will take to put things right for them. In this situation, questions you can ask are:

- 'What will put this right for you?'
- 'How do you want me to help you?'
- 'How can we move this forward?'
- 'What would you like to happen next?'
- 'How can we best resolve this?'

React positively and reach a solution

When you have established all the facts, it could be that you can reach a resolution with the customer if the complaint is a simple one and you have undertaken a thorough investigation. Sometimes you may need to investigate further and come back to the customer when you have investigated the facts.

In any event, in this stage of the conversation it is important that you react positively with the customer. Telling the customer what is not possible or why you cannot do something for them will not help resolve the situation; it can give a negative impression and make the customer angry. Choose your words carefully and remember to use positive language. For example: 'Certainly, I will be able to speak to him about this tomorrow. How does that sound to you?' is much more positive than saying: 'I'll try and speak to him today but I can't guarantee I will be able to get hold of him until tomorrow. OK?'

Table 6.1 gives a list of words that create a positive impression with the customer and those that don't. It is important to emphasize to the customer what you can do to solve the situation, not what you can't.

There may however be occasions when you cannot do what the customer asks. Avoid using phrases such as: 'It's not our policy.' This can appear aggressive and unhelpful to the customer. What you can do in this situation is empathize with the customer and clearly explain the reasoning behind the decision. Stress what is possible rather than what is not, and check that this is OK with the customer; for example 'I appreciate it is frustrating having to give us your policy details. The reason we have to do this is to comply with data protection rules and to protect your personal account details. What I can do is accept any ID such as your full name, first line of your address and month of your birth. Then I will be able to access the information straight away. Is that OK with you?'

TABLE 6.1 Positive and negative words

Positive words	Negative words
Can	Can't
Will	Won't
Yes	No
Now	Never
Certainly	Unfortunately
Definitely	Difficulty
Situation	Problem
Guarantee	Doubt
Know	Unaware
Ensure	Try
Confirm	Can't confirm
Best	Worst
Immediately	Later
I'm sure	I'm afraid
A pleasure	No worries

Notify the customer of the action and note what is to be done

Once you have come to an agreement with the customer about the action you will take, make sure that both of you are clear what will happen next. Confirm the actions and ensure that you make a note of this on your complaint-management system.

Take action

Importantly, keep your promises. If you say you will come back to the customer by a certain time for example, make sure that you do this. Follow through on your promises.

If you apply all six steps when handling a complaint, you will have LEARNT from the situation and recovered the customer's loyalty and trust (Figure 6.1).

FIGURE 6.1 The LEARNT process for dealing with complaints

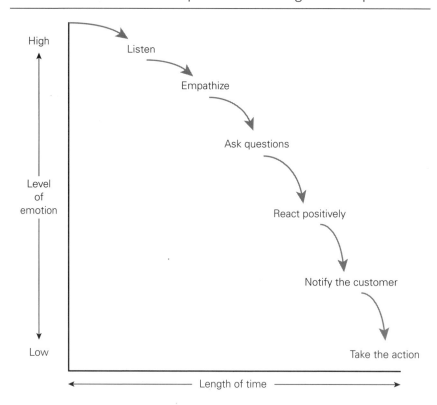

Dealing with complaints in writing

In order to ensure a speedy reply to a complaint, best practice is to pick up the phone to the customer. Nevertheless, there may be times when you are unable to reach the customer by phone or when you need to write a response letter to the customer. In many market sectors regulatory requirements set out a timescale for written responses.

My experience is that the standard of letter writing has declined in recent years, not helped by the widespread use of text-speak. As a result, more organizations are turning to the use of letter templates to make it easier for customer-service agents to write response letters. This is fine as long as the agent remembers to delete the parts of the letter template that are not relevant to the customer. I received a letter recently that included the instructions to the agent for completing the template, which the agent had not deleted!

Every organization will have its own house style and tone of communication. I am a great believer in the use of plain English in all written correspondence so the message is crystal clear. Sadly, it seems that some letter writers feel that as soon as they put pen to paper, they need to adopt a lengthy, bureaucratic way of speaking.

Here are two letters, both from the same company, that I received some time ago when I complained about a rail journey. The train that I was on broke down in a tunnel and I and other passengers had to wait for four hours without heat or electricity before we could continue with our journey.

Not only is the language rather bureaucratic in both letters, but both are clearly standard letters with no personalization or reference to my specific complaint. Furthermore the letters both contain jargon.

The first letter acknowledges my complaint but gives no timeline for when the company will write again. In addition I find the second letter is full of justification and excuses about why the situation occurred. This does not reassure me as a customer.

Dear Mrs Cook

We acknowledge receipt of your complaint following your recent journey with us and we are sorry to hear your experience of our service was not to the expected standard.

Please be assured that we treat all complaints on every aspect of our service with the utmost seriousness and we are investigating the matter on your behalf.

A response containing an explanation will follow in due course. In the meantime, please accept our apologies, on behalf of all of us for the poor impression received.

Yours sincerely
pp.
Miss Carol Trent
Customer Response Unit Supervisor

Two months later I received the following letter:

Dear Mrs Cook

In the recent months of or our operation there have been delays and disruptions which have resulted in inconvenience to our passengers. The teething troubles we have encountered have affected availability of rolling stock, which in turn has disrupted our scheduled running and affected our ability, at times to transport passengers within an acceptable timescale.

You have sent in a complaint following your journey either be completing one of our complaints forms, telephoning our office, or following up in writing. Our normal procedure is to acknowledge complaints on receipt and then follow up with a detailed explanation for the inconvenience you have been caused, responding to each complaint with a personal reply.

However, the level of feedback received has resulted in our standards not being met and our customers further inconvenienced with a delay in our response. In view of this, we have taken the decision to provide a general answer to your complaint. We sincerely apologize if any individual comments or enquiries have not been met and hope that our response will be satisfactory in the circumstances.

The majority of comments received have been regarding delays and subsequent lack of information. Teething troubles with our rolling stock and signalling systems have been the main reason for delays. The flow of information to our customers is recognized as being of paramount importance and many improvements are being made to ensure that information is available at all times. Improved Passenger Information Boards are being installed in the departure stations and there are plans for a similar facility across the network. We normally supply up to the minute information on the status of departures and we will soon be better equipped to advise of current timetabling, giving customers an opportunity to wait in our lounge or assess the effect of a delay on their travel plans.

We do envisage that once our fleet of rolling stock has been fully commissioned and our systems are all functioning correctly departures waiting times will be minimized to an acceptable level.

Please be assured we are working hard to improve our service and meet customers' expectations. Thank you again for writing. Please be assured that your comments have been noted and included in our Operations Division's plans for future improvements to our service. We apologize for the poor impression you received and we look forward to an opportunity of welcoming you back to our service in the very near future.

Yours sincerely
John Smythe
Customer-service Manager

Writing style

In terms of writing style, plain English helps build rapport with the customer and encourage confidence and trust. Here are some tips that you can apply:

- The start of the letter sets the tone for what follows. It's best not to use expressions such as: 'I acknowledge receipt of...', 'We are in receipt of...', 'I am writing in reference to...', 'With reference to...', 'We thank you for...'

  'Thank you for...' is the best approach.

  Likewise do not head the letter with lengthy references – these can appear official and un-customer-friendly. Match the form of address that customers use to refer to themselves in the letter. So, for example if the customer has signed herself 'Doris Lessing (Mrs)', do not address her as 'Doris' but rather 'Mrs Lessing'. Where you are not sure about the marital status of a lady customer, address her as 'Ms'.

- A good rule of thumb is one sentence equals one point. You should aim for a maximum of 20 words in a sentence. If you have more, then you can probably break it down into two main parts. Look for joining words such as 'and', 'but', 'therefore' and 'however'. This is a good indication of where you can put a full stop.

- Use 'I' throughout the letter, as in: 'I have spoken to the store', rather than 'we'. This is unless you are referring to the organization (for example 'We have a store in your local town').

- Use words you use in everyday language but avoid slang. People sometimes try to make their written language too formal. Ironically, you lose authority if you try to sound important. Avoid using jargon that you might understand but may mean nothing to the customer. (An example in the second letter above is the mention of 'rolling stock'.) Don't use slang or colloquialisms: 'What happened is a right pain' is not the same as 'This has created problems'.

- Don't try to sound clever by using long words when short words will do. Examples of this rule are using the word 'need' instead of 'requirement', 'later' instead of 'subsequent'. Another tip is always to ensure that you have an active verb in the sentence. 'The cat sat on the mat' is far easier to understand than the passive version: 'the mat was sat on by the cat.'

Structuring a written response

If you send a letter to acknowledge a customer's complaint, make sure that this includes clear timelines for when you intend to come back with a resolution. It is also essential to take ownership of the letter and let the customer know who you are, and when and how to contact you if necessary.

The structure of a complaint resolution letter will vary from organization to organization. Best practice is to ensure you include in your resolution letter:

- a thank you to the customer for their call/e-mail/letter/post;
- a paragraph saying sorry and expressing empathy;
- your understanding of what the complaint was about, ensuring you address all the customer's concerns;
- details of the investigations and what you have found out;

- whether you agree that the complaint is justified or not, and why this is;

- how you propose to remedy the situation;

- details of any redress (financial or non-financial) that you intend to make, and when.

If you work in a regulated environment, you will also need to include reference to the relevant independent arbitration services.

Importantly, before you send any correspondence, check it for quality. It sometimes helps if an independent person sense-checks your mail. As well as following the structural guidelines that I outlined above, ensure that your grammar, spelling and punctuation are correct and that you have spelt the customer's name correctly. The customer will quickly lose confidence in the organization if any of this is incorrect or if the tone is not professional and friendly.

Key learning points

- The LEARNT six-step process allows complaint handlers to respond to complaints effectively face to face or on the telephone.

- When writing to customers, use plain English, good grammar, punctuation and spelling, and adopt an approachable tone.

- Structure your letter so that it addresses all the customer's issues, showing what investigations you have carried out, your conclusions as well as any remedial action and redress.

Recording and thoroughly investigating complaints

07

Although this chapter is a short one, it is important. In it I outline the essential need to record all complaint data. I also outline why it is important to thoroughly investigate a complaint and how to ensure that you address all the customer's issues before arriving at a decision.

Recording complaints

It is a sad fact of human nature that employees often simply ignore or minimize complaints. One study of an unnamed supermarket chain found that members of staff and their team leaders tended to 'fob off' customers who complained, saying things like: 'You're absolutely right, I'll report it straight away' and then doing nothing about it. In addition they admitted being selective in the complaints that they did report – screening out those that they did not think important or where complaints were about work colleagues.

In one customer-service department we have come across, complaint handlers who received complaints about their colleagues in the sales department were expected to report them and the colleague concerned would then have money directly taken off their bonus. Little wonder complaints of this nature were frequently not reported but instead were suppressed. In another large company, the focus on sales, coupled with the lack of staff and out-of-date systems that were disparate across the organization, led to complaints not being recorded or investigated thoroughly. Customers did not receive a fair outcome to their complaint and consequently the firm received a heavy fine from the regulator.

I find that not recording a complaint is generally a symptom of two things: a poor attitude to complaint handling and customer service generally, and lack of an efficient and effective complaint-handling system.

Later I talk about how to engage staff and encourage them to take ownership of a complaint. I also cover how to give feedback, for example to people who do not take ownership of a complaint. In the final chapter I talk about complaint handling and organizational culture, and how the culture affects people's attitudes to the customer. Recording all complaints allows an organization to get the information it needs to improve and to rebuild the relationship with the customer, so it is worthwhile investing in a proprietary complaint-management system that is easy to use and accessible to all.

An effective complaint-management system:

- enables you to thoroughly record the complaint;
- enables you to monitor the efficiency and effectiveness of the complaint resolution;
- allows you to collate management information about complaints;
- permits swift identification and response when complaints need to be reported to other departments or companies in the distribution network, or to law-enforcement or regulatory agencies;
- allows you to identify root causes;
- provides market research through revealing complaint trends.

At Southern Ohio Medical Centre in the United States, a new complaint-management system allowed the hospital to dramatically improve the way it handled its complaints. Before the installation of the CDC complaint-management software system, complaints were logged manually, customer letters and files were often mislaid while passing between departments, and management had little access to data on root causes of complaints. The new system, which allowed centralized recording of complaints and scanning of customer documentation, reduced complaint-response times to below seven days, streamlining information between departments and allowing managers easier access to complaints data.

To ensure that all expressions of dissatisfaction are logged, insurance company CIS in the UK has introduced a centralized, automated system for recording complaints and reporting to the Financial Services Authority (FSA). Centralizing the complaints-handling process has provided CIS with a single view of each complaint, facilitating a more comprehensive approach to complaint management.

Now the complaint is categorized by both CIS department and policy type for internal tracking purposes, and by the FSA reporting class for regulatory reasons. This ensures consistency of data across the organization and makes it easier for management to collate the information and analyse customer-service performance. Reports in the regulatory format are built into the system and can be generated and presented whenever the FSA requires the information.

CIS claims to have made savings in labour costs (and improvements in operational efficiency of over 2,000 customer-facing staff) and filing space (estimated at £100,000 per annum).

One of the issues that many companies face is the wide range of customer feedback that they receive. This can often result in paralysis – the business is overwhelmed by the various data feeds it receives as feedback and fails to develop a plan of action to implement improvement. Having a robust complaint-management system can overcome this.

Travel company British Airways Holidays uses one system to log the entire customer experience – from pre- to post-travel. As well as capturing customer complaints and compliments, it stores feedback from agents and suppliers around the world. The system provides 'one view' of the whole customer journey. In this way the company is able to identify potential areas of dissatisfaction at each of the customer touch points and take improvement action accordingly.

In Ireland, the Children's University Hospital in Temple Street, Dublin has made its complaints-management system accessible at ward and departmental level by rolling it out across the hospital. It has seen an increase in the incidents recorded on the system, ranging from complaints and compliments to patient queries and clinical and non-clinical liability cases. This has provided the hospital with better-quality information that has helped it more easily identify where improvements are needed. It has also helped it be compliant with the Irish Health Act regulatory requirements.

Accuracy of logging

Complaint details need to be recorded accurately. A good test of this is to imagine that another customer-service professional who knows nothing about the case had to take it over. Would he or she be able to do this based on the case notes you had provided? Notes recorded on the system need to be factual, accurate and concise.

In particular, ensure that all aspects of the complaint are recorded. Take my own recent experience as an example. I dropped off my car at valet parking at the airport, and on my return I discovered that its paintwork had been scratched. When I reported this to the company, the person I spoke to at the airport was dismissive. He promised to call me back, having looked at their video recording to see what had happened in the airport and failed to do so. When I complained to the company it was about two things: first, the scratch on my car and, second, the poor attitude of the member of staff. The letter I received in response addressed only the first problem: the scratch on my car. The company ignored the other aspect of my complaint. In my mind the complaint had not been accurately logged and therefore the investigation of my complaint was incomplete.

Why investigate thoroughly?

To deal with a complaint in a fair and timely fashion, complaint handlers need to undertake a thorough investigation.

Calling the customer to discuss the complaint situation demonstrates a genuine interest in the customer's concerns. It also allows you to gain a more in-depth understanding of the customer's issue/s. It is essential also to investigate staff and third parties' recollection of events and to consult relevant documentation such as product or company information.

In every complaint situation, the complaint handler needs to make a decision about whether each issue regarding the complaint is upheld (ie, found in favour of the customer) or not. Decision making will not be fair and impartial unless the complaint handler has all the facts. You will need to explain the rationale for the decision about the complaint to the customer. You can only know what decision to make when you have collected all the evidence that will prove what the actual situation is. Unless the complaint handler investigates all the issues, he or she is unlikely to arrive at a fair conclusion for the customer.

Consider all elements of the complaint, as well as any personal impact the error has had on the customer. It is good to involve the customer in the resolution by asking: 'What would put this right for you?'

Don't forget, there are also other benefits of thorough investigation. It helps you:

- to discover the root cause of the complaint;
- to ensure the complaint is resolved satisfactorily without being re-opened;
- to minimize the likelihood of future errors and complaints from other customers.

Investigation checklist

Every organization will have various channels that the complaint handler will need to investigate in order to gather evidence. It is important that the complaint handler knows where to go to find the facts.

Here is a useful checklist to help ensure that the complaint is investigated thoroughly:

- What is the complaint about?
- What specific issues has the customer raised?
- When did the complaint situation occur?
- Who specifically was involved in the situation?
- What does the customer say happened?
- Who have you contacted about the complaint?

- What is the staff member's version of the event/s?
- What are third parties' recollections of the event/s (where relevant)?
- What relevant product or company information have you consulted and what does this tell you?
- What other evidence have you gathered?
- What is your conclusion about how the complaint situation occurred?
- Why did it occur?
- What decision have you made about whether the complainant's issue/s should be upheld?
- What does the customer want you to do as a result of the complaint?
- What remedial action do you need to take?
- What redress do you need to offer if appropriate?
- What have you done to prevent the complaint recurring?
- Have you recorded all the above details on the complaint-management system?

Explain the outcome

Once complaint handlers have thoroughly investigated complaints, ideally they should contact the customers by phone to let them know about the investigation, what has been decided about the complaint, and the reasons why. Calling the customer allows the customer-service professional to gain the customer's agreement on the way forward, and then to confirm what has been agreed in writing. Customers may not always like the business's decision about the complaint, but they should be able to understand that the organization has arrived at a fair outcome after a thorough investigation.

Sometimes an apology and a promise to put matters right are not enough to resolve a complaint. You may need to apply either financial or non-financial redress if the organization has made an error. This can be a refund, replacement or exchange. You may need to reimburse or compensate the customer or, if the organization has not made an error, to offer a financial or non-financial gesture of goodwill. In all instances it is important to act fairly and quickly to follow through on promises. Always keep the customer informed about what will happen next and when.

Key learning points

- Encourage everyone to record complaints on a central complaint system in a thorough and accurate manner.

- Ensure you establish all the facts so the complaint can be investigated thoroughly and assessed fairly.

- Identify and use all the information available to understand what happened, including speaking to the customer, reviewing relevant documentation, and speaking to colleagues or third parties in order to arrive at a fair and impartial decision.

Conciliation, mediation and arbitration

08

If complaints cannot be resolved directly between the customer and the organization, they can be referred to third-party dispute resolution. In this chapter I discuss what conciliation, mediation and arbitration are. I then go on to look at mediation skills that complaint handlers can adopt in-house when dealing with complex, escalated or re-opened complaints.

Conciliation, mediation and arbitration

If a customer and an organization cannot come to a mutually acceptable agreement, either party can use the services of unbiased individuals or panels to resolve disputes through conciliation, mediation and arbitration.

- Conciliation is where a neutral conciliator brings the parties together and encourages them to find a mutually acceptable resolution to the dispute.

- Mediation is when a neutral mediator becomes actively involved in discussions between the parties. The mediator can propose a resolution, but cannot dictate a settlement of the dispute.

- Arbitration is when an independent individual or panel hears the facts on both sides of a dispute and reaches a decision, which in most cases both parties will previously have agreed to accept. However, in some instances, such as regulatory environments, it is just the organization that has to abide by the independent decision.

A small percentage of customers who complain seek more formal third-party complaint resolution in small-claims courts. Use of the courts can be cumbersome and costly for both sides, and can usually be avoided if efforts are made in good faith to resolve disputes at the company level or through informal dispute resolution.

Mediation

Mediation is becoming increasingly popular across sectors as a method for resolving more complex complaints. It can also be used prior to a formal complaint, as this advert from Salisbury NHS Trust promotes:

Mediation can be used to resolve conflict/communication breakdown between patients/relatives and staff to stop the situation from escalating to a formal complaint. In some cases a complaint investigation may be under way already. If this is the case, the mediator's role is purely to mediate between the parties to restore communication. The mediator will not be involved in the investigation of the complaint.

Mediation does not always have to be undertaken by a specialist external body. I have seen an increase in the number of specialist complaint handlers, such as people working in executive-response teams, who are undertaking mediation training. This is because specialist complaint handlers often sit between the customer and the business. Their role is to ensure that accurate, honest information is received from both the customer and the business about the circumstances of the complaint, enabling a fair assessment and decision to be made. By the time the specialist receives the complaint, both sides may have failed to arrive at an agreement, so the specialist's role is to help the parties reach a settlement. In this sense it is assisted complaint handling. It helps the two parties in conflict to bridge difficulties.

A mediator seeks to enable both parties to reach forward-looking solutions by consensus.

Mediation is useful in a wide variety of conflicts, particularly in the complaint situation, at the point when emotions have eased enough that the parties can begin to negotiate. It achieves an impartial and fair outcome.

Where mediation adds value

Mediation can add value in a number of complaint situations:

- when there is deadlock around a complaint;
- when there are difficult factual issues;
- when the issues are complicated by a strong emotional element;
- when publicity is not desirable;
- when continuing the relationship with the customer is important;
- when the organization would prefer the customer not to refer the complaint to independent arbitration.

Mediation gives people the chance to air their grievances. Intense conflict tends to generate misunderstanding and suspicion; many of these evaporate when the parties are able to express their views.

When mediation is not appropriate

Mediation will not be successful if:

- The complaint is very serious and the customer is still too upset to discuss the situation.
- The customer wants to keep the conflict going.
- You suspect that mediation is going to be used to escalate the dispute.
- The complaint issues are, in your judgement, insurmountable.

Conflict management

As we have seen, in any complaint situation, there is a degree of emotion. High emotions lead to potential conflict situations. The role of the mediator in these situations is to attempt to work with the other person to find some solution that fully satisfies the concerns of both parties.

What makes a good mediator?

The personal characteristics and skills that are particularly valuable in mediation are similar to those of the complaint handler, such as strong listening and questioning skills and the ability to empathize. There are also other characteristics such as

- patience;
- the ability to be comfortable with high emotion, arguments and interruptions;
- the ability to influence;
- impartiality: putting aside one's own opinions and reactions, and being able to withhold judgement.

Impartiality

One of the key skills of the mediator is being impartial. Our senses bombard us with two billion bits of information per second but our conscious mind can only deal with between five and nine at any given moment. Therefore an awful lot of information is filtered out. This filtration process is influenced by our personal values and beliefs, memories, decisions and experiences, and our cultural and social background. This helps us to allow in only the information our filters are tuned to receive.

What this means is that each of us has a very individual map of our world. To be an effective mediator, it is a really useful exercise to attempt to understand the internal reality or map of the other person with whom you are communicating. Impartiality means that while listening to someone you put aside thoughts of what the person should do, whether they are right or wrong, and what you would have done in the situation. You truly listen to speakers, both the content of what they are saying and the emotions they are conveying. You are not thinking about defending your position or how to respond. Your focus is on understanding people's perception of the complaint situation.

This means having a clear mind and not thinking about resolutions too quickly. Think:

- What assumptions am I making when dealing with this customer?
- What am I telling myself inside my head that is stopping me truly listening and understanding this person's point of view?

The mediation process

Imagine that you have been handed a complex complaint that has been escalated to you from another part of the business. The case has been re-opened because the customer disputes the findings of the complaint investigation and has added supplementary information about the case. The complaint is not about you or the direct area of business in which you work (both of these conditions would make it impossible to mediate).

There are five phases to the mediation process:

1. Opening the conversation

As in a standard complaint situation, the first step is to call the customer. During the opening phase of the mediation process, seek to establish that the customer is willing to discuss the issues and it is convenient for him or her to talk.

Explain that you are taking responsibility for dealing with the complaint. Remember, you will have prepared for the call. For the customer this may be the first time they have spoken directly to someone dealing with the problem. It could be appropriate to write to the customer beforehand to say that you will phone. Alternatively you may need to fix a time to call back to give the customer the opportunity to collect his or her thoughts.

- Create rapport with the customer and emphasize that you are here to help resolve their concerns.
- Remember to separate the problem from the person.
- Always show the customer respect, courtesy, patience and tolerance.

2. Clarification

During the clarification stage of the call, the mediator uses the opportunity to gain a better understanding of the issues surrounding the complaint from the customer's perspective. He or she will refer to the points that the customer made in other communications and seek examples, explanations and clarification of the issues. Importantly the mediator ends this phase with a summary of what the customer has said, acknowledging their interests and concerns.

Empathy is a powerful technique that allows the mediator to appreciate the emotional distress a situation may have caused whilst still maintaining impartiality. As we have seen, empathy needs to be sincere. By naming the emotion that the customer is feeling, the mediator builds a bridge towards a solution.

Likewise there may be occasions when the organization has made a mistake and it is appropriate to apologize. If this is the case, the effective mediator ensures that the apology it offers is sincere. Phrases such as:

'I am *really* sorry that this has happened'

'I do *truly* apologize for the inconvenience'

are far more powerful than

'I can only apologize.'

3. The exchange

After the customer's issues have been clarified, the exchange phase is where the mediator discusses the firm's response and/or answers the customer's issues from the business's perspective.

This could lead to some uncomfortable emotions, challenges, and opposing perspectives. During this phase the gap between the parties can seem very wide and this is often the most anxious time in the mediation process. Expect customers to need significant time to air their grievances before they are emotionally ready to accept a potential resolution.

Occasionally, after an intense exchange, there is a moment we call the 'turning point'. The mediator empathizes with the customer on behalf of the business, or maybe offers a concession or a kind word. The customer falls silent. Then he or she may begin sharing more information and become more accepting of the business's point of view.

4. Agreement

During the agreement phase of the mediation the complaint handler outlines any potential or agreed resolutions or remedial actions. Even if a resolution has not been achieved on the telephone, the mediator summarizes both parties' perspectives and outlines any potential next steps.

5. Close

Ideally the close of the call should leave the customer with a positive impression of the organization. Even if the mediator has not managed to fully resolve the issue from the customer's perspective, the process will have hopefully enhanced the customer's perception of the organization by showing that it is willing to listen and recognize the customer's issues, as well as by offering an explanation of the business's perspective.

Questioning techniques

Questioning allows the mediator to discover more about what the customer is thinking and feeling as well as what would be acceptable to them to resolve their concerns. When mediating, listen carefully for people's interests – what really matters to them. Also ask the customer's permission to take notes; this shows you are actively listening and engaged.

Here are examples of questions that you may find useful for each phase of the mediation process:

1. Opening the conversation

Examples:

'When is a convenient time to speak?'

'Thank you for writing. So I can help resolve your complaint, please tell me more about what happened from your perspective.'

'I have read your letter thoroughly. To move things forward, please tell me some more background information.'

2. Clarify

Examples:

'From your letter I can see that you have concerns about... and... Is that correct?'

'What concerns you about the situation?'

'How does... affect you?'

'Tell me more about...'

'Can you give me an example?'

'Please explain...'

'Please help me understand what...'

'What is it you think that we don't understand about the situation?'

'Tell me what happened when...'

3. Exchange (having given the organization's view)

Examples:

'How can we move this forward?'

'Is there some way we can meet both your need for... and our need for...?'

'What's the next step in your mind?'

'What might work for you?'

'What can we do to help resolve this issue?'

'What would be the best solution for both of us?'

'What would make this idea work better for you?'

'What would you be comfortable with?'

4. Agree

Examples:

'Is this solution acceptable to you?'

'Have we covered everything?'

'What aspect of this are you uneasy with?'

5. Close

Examples:

'I'll be writing to confirm this telephone conversation. Are you happy with this?'

'Is there anything else I can do for you?'

Influencing techniques

Here are some tips from trained mediators on how you can influence the customer and move the situation forward in a positive manner. You are more likely to gain the customer's agreement to the views/actions you are proposing if you adopt one of the following influencing techniques:

- Support the organization's views and position with up to two key facts or reasons (any more than this, your message gets lost): for example 'We have to ask you to do this because...' or 'We can offer you... because...'

- Describe the benefits of the proposed course of action: for example 'The advantages of this course of action are...', 'the benefits are...'
- Provide incentives for doing something: for example 'If you do this, we will be able to...'
- State the consequences of not doing something: for example 'If you do not do this, we will have to...'

When you have stated your position, *pause*. Using a pause:

- gives you time to formulate the right words;
- adds emphasis to what you say;
- allows the customer time to think before answering.

Mediation skills criteria

Here is a checklist that we use as part of our complaint-handling mediation training that I hope you will find useful:

Mediation phases and skills

Open
Checks that it is convenient for the customer to speak
Creates rapport
Emphasizes he or she is there to help
Explains they are taking responsibility for the customer's complaint

Clarify
Asks open questions
Seeks examples and explanations
Acknowledges the interests and concerns heard
Apologizes/demonstrates empathy where appropriate
Listens intuitively

Mediation phases and skills

Exchange

Clearly explains the organization's position
Allows silence
Manages high emotions, arguments and interruptions appropriately
Displays impartiality
Listens intuitively
Influences appropriately
Works to a joint solution
Discusses details of resolution if appropriate

Agree

Summarizes both parties' perspectives (even if resolution not agreed)
Confirms resolutions or actions agreed
Outlines any potential next steps

Close

Leaves the customer with a positive impression of the business
Confirms details of the call will be sent in writing

Key learning points

- Mediation is increasingly being used when complaints are complex, escalated or re-opened.

- There are five phases to the mediation process. Key to applying them well is to remain impartial.

Will you make a good mediator?

This inventory will allow you to assess the way you deal with challenging situations. It will give you an indicator of whether you will be a good mediator.

Read each statement and give each a score according to how characteristic the statement is of you.

Score:

5 = completely characteristic of you = I always do this/Yes

4 = usually characteristic of you = I usually do this

3 = somewhat characteristic of you = I do this sometimes

2 = usually uncharacteristic = I usually do not do this

1 = completely uncharacteristic = I never do this/No

1 I always empathize with a customer's situation even if I think they are being unreasonable.

2 When faced with an angry customer I prefer to pass them on to a colleague to deal with.

3 I relieve tension at work by making fun of customers behind their backs.

4 I make sure customers know that I am more knowledgeable than them.

5 I do not have difficulty demonstrating an interest in what the customer is saying.

6 I promise to do things for customers that I can't always fulfil to stop them complaining.

7 When people annoy me, I say nothing, but show my annoyance through my body language.

8 When customers are being unreasonable I fight the organization's corner.

9 I take responsibility for owning a complaint, even if it's not directly my fault.

10 When I've promised something for a customer and I haven't managed to do it, I avoid getting back to them.

11 In a difficult situation I use sarcasm to deflate the situation.

12 If customers are rude to me, I am not afraid to be rude back.

13 I stay calm when dealing with challenging customers.

14 I feel embarrassed to raise issues with my line manager.

15 When people take advantage of me, I silently even the score.

16 If I have something to say that I think is important, I will interrupt a customer or colleague.

17 I identify who can resolve a complaint if I can't.

18 I want everyone to like me.

19 When a customer has been awkward I take my time to follow through.

20 I let the customer know if they are in the wrong.

21 I always tell the customer what we can do, not what we can't do.

22 I tend to give in to customers and colleagues and do what they want.

23 I blame other people when things go wrong.

24 I stare people down.

25 I check that customers are happy with the proposed actions to resolve their complaint.

26 I don't like to draw attention to myself by going that extra mile.

27 When customers complain, I do my best to get rid of them.

28 I like to be in control of every situation.

29 I record a complaint completely and accurately from start to finish.

30 I find it difficult to ask questions in a challenging situation.

31 I take complaints in my stride as it's only a job.

32 When I am having a bad day customers and colleagues know it.

33 I appreciate that handling a customer complaint empathetically and competently is an opportunity to develop customer loyalty.

34 I have difficulty maintaining eye contact with others.

35 I let my colleagues know if they come to serve a customer who has complained in the past.

36 I quote policy to get customers to understand.

37 I believe in treating each customer with integrity and fairness.

38 I do not like to say things directly that might hurt people's feelings.

39 I call in favours when I need to get something done.

40 I raise my voice or use hand gestures to make myself understood.

How to score

Write your score for only the following statements in the box below:

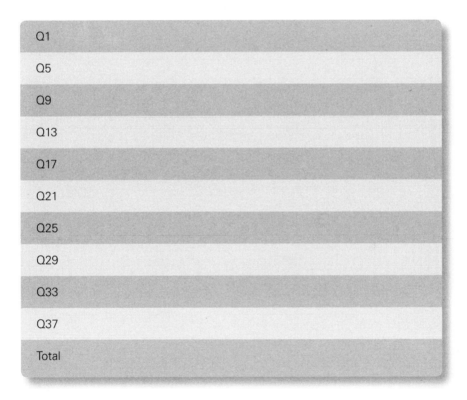

Q1	
Q5	
Q9	
Q13	
Q17	
Q21	
Q25	
Q29	
Q33	
Q37	
Total	

Now total your score for these statements. If you have a score of 45 and above, you will make a good mediator.

Making improvements as a result of complaints

09

I n this chapter I address the benefits that can be gained via robust root-cause analysis in making improvements. I also cover:

- problem-solving techniques;
- service-improvement plans;
- communicating results to customers.

Learning from complaints

It is easy when handling complaints to become bogged down in day-to-day case management and forget one of the overriding benefits of complaints: they provide the organization with information to help it improve.

AXA Insurance provides financial protection to over 515 million clients worldwide and has 110,000 employees. In the UK complaints are handled at a business level, and if necessary escalated to a centralized customer care team. AXA receives over 1,000 complaints a month across a variety of business units. It analyses complaints data to identify strategic and tactical trends, and actively seeks to implement improvements. For example, customer feedback around the Auto Engineering Service has enabled AXA to remove three days from the average turnaround time of a vehicle being repaired.

This has resulted in considerable improvements in efficiency and cost savings while also improving the customer experience.

The benefits of root-cause analysis

Root-cause analysis involves treating the causes of complaints – rather than dealing with the symptoms on a repeated basis, which leads to increasing frustration for employees and customers alike. For example, businesses encourage staff to record complaints on their complaint-management system. The person who records the complaint has various options to select to indicate the root cause.

Having done this, and investigated and resolved the complaint, the person dealing with it typically hears nothing further from the overall owner of the complaint-management system about what has happened to prevent further complaints of this nature occurring.

Root-cause analysis involves gathering and analysing customer data in order to establish the 'voice of the customer'. As a result of analysis, the business can then identify key improvement trends and emerging issues. This allows it to develop and implement service-improvement plans. Importantly, once change has been made, the organization needs to keep customers informed of improvements. This affirms their commitment to being a customer-focused business.

Root-cause analysis can help businesses identify improvements in their products and services. It also provides useful data to help develop new products and services, and identify blockages in processes so that the system can be made more efficient and effective. It also indicates training needs.

Root-cause analysis is dependent on good-quality data that is reliable and consistent and maintained by robust systems and processes.

Service-improvement activity should be a senior management responsibility

If your organization really intends to take complaints seriously, make sure that complaints' MI, root-cause analysis and service improvement are regular topics on your senior management agenda. Private bank Coutts, for example, has a service-improvement board made up of senior managers and members of the customer-relations team, who meet on a monthly basis to review issues and monitor service improvements.

Pareto principle

The 80/20 rule, called the Pareto principle after the Italian economist who proposed it, relates to the fact that typically 80 per cent of your organization's customer complaints will relate to 20 per cent of the service that a business or function may provide. By identifying the key areas of customer dissatisfaction via complaints and tackling these, businesses can increase their overall levels of customer satisfaction and loyalty.

Best-practice customer-service organizations deploy analysts to use complaints data to produce management information. This typically identifies the major causes of complaints, overall trends and emerging issues. Outputs can be tracked on a regular basis to monitor patterns over time. Many organizations also have teams who analyse complaints that have been referred to ombudsman services for external arbitration. The in-house teams track trends and external judgements affecting the industry so that they can make improvements. Typically an organization will incur a cost or penalty when this happens, so apart from anything else it is in its interest to learn from external judgements about complaints so as to avoid similar cases being referred to an ombudsman service.

Techniques you can use for root-cause analysis

In this section I outline some useful problem-solving techniques that you and your team can use to create a robust service-improvement plan. This is based on the four-stage process shown in Figure 9.1.

You will see the stage I am going to focus on most is the first: defining the problem. If the service professional does not define exactly why there is a complaint issue around a particular topic area, then any improvement activity will be targeted at the incorrect solution. So for example, you may have a large number of complaints about mis-selling a product to customers. There

FIGURE 9.1 Four-stage service-improvement process

1. Define the problem
(Analyse the root causes of the problem)

2. Generate options for improvement
(Identify possible solutions via brainstorming and benchmarking)

3. Evaluate options
(Select the best improvement solution)

4. Implement the improvement
(Gain acceptance, develop a service-improvement plan,
implement the plan, review effectiveness and communicate
success to customers and employees)

may be many potential causes: incorrect sales script, lack of staff training, sales incentive systems that drive unhelpful behaviour and so on. The temptation, when looking at areas to improve, is to dive straight in at Stage 2 of the process, generating options for improvement, without understanding the true issues.

Techniques for defining the problem

Best practice is to use the management information you obtain from complaints and form a team to develop service improvements. Here are three methods to help you define the root causes of a complaint before the team starts generating ideas:

- problem checklist;
- why, why, why, why, why;
- fishbone diagram.

Problem checklist

A problem checklist allows the complaint owner to consider all aspects of the problem in order to arrive at a definition of the underlying causes. This helps ensure he or she understands the background to the problem. To use the checklist, ask the person who 'owns' the problem – that is, the person responsible for the aspect of the product or service you are discussing – to be present at the meeting.

Ask the problem owner the following questions:

- What is the problem?
- When does the problem occur?
- How does the problem occur?
- Why does the problem occur?
- Who does the problem impact on?
- How often does it impact on them?
- How does it affect them?
- Where does the problem originate?
- What is causing the problem?
- Who is causing the problem?
- What are the constraints in solving the problem? (eg money, time, resources).
- When does the problem need to be resolved?
- What will happen if the problem is not resolved?

Once the team has listened to the responses, they need to write a statement defining the problem, beginning with the phrase: 'The issue we need to improve is how to...'

In this way everyone will be aware of the background to the problem and what you are trying to achieve.

The 'five whys'

The 'five whys' is a question-asking method used to explore the cause-and-effect relationships underlying a particular problem. Ultimately, the goal of applying the five-whys method is to determine a root cause of a defect or problem. The technique is very simple to use and involves asking a series of 'Why?' questions. The following example demonstrates the basic process:

I have a problem: my car will not start.

1 Why? The battery is dead (first why).

2 Why? The alternator is not functioning (second why).

3 Why? The alternator has broken beyond repair (third why).

4 Why? The alternator is well beyond its useful service life and has never been replaced (fourth why).

5 Why? I have not been maintaining my car according to the recommended service schedule (fifth why; this is the root cause).

You may not need to ask five 'why' iterations but this is generally sufficient to get to a root cause. The real key is to avoid assumptions and instead to trace the chain of causality in direct increments from the effect to the first problem to the root cause.

Fishbone diagrams

Fishbone diagrams, often also called cause-and-effect diagrams, are useful because they enable team members to use their personal knowledge to categorize the causes of the problem. They help provide ideas about the root causes of a problem. These can then be further quantified using complaint-management data.

The fishbone diagram breaks down a problem or an effect into its component parts. The causes of the problem are categorized so that the completed diagram looks like the skeleton of a fish.

To complete the diagram:

1 Write the problem or effect in a box on the right-hand side of a flipchart. Draw a large arrow across the sheet pointing to it.

2 Draw arrows indicating the main categories and pointing toward the central arrow at an angle.

3 The main categories are typically People, Process, Systems and Environment, but others may be used. It is not important where the cause is categorized as long as it appears on the diagram.

4 As a group, brainstorm the causes that relate to each category.

FIGURE 9.2 Example of a fishbone diagram

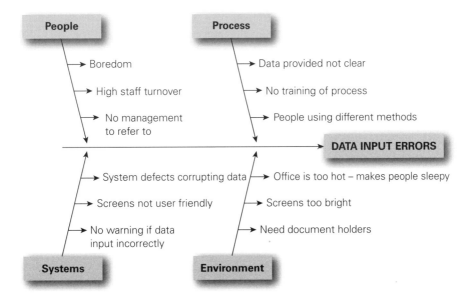

5 You may need to take a category and break down the details further via brainstorming.

6 Look for the category that has the biggest number of causes. Consider what further evidence you may need to gather in order to substantiate or quantify the causes in this category.

7 When you have identified the biggest causes, consider what corrective action you can take to minimize the effect of these causes, in this way solving the problem.

Figure 9.2 shows a completed fishbone diagram for complaints that have been received around a high level of data input errors amongst a sales administration team.

Generating options for improvement

Once you have defined the root cause(s) of the problem, involve the improvement team in generating ideas for improvement. Brainstorming has a few rules that make it effective and fun. Here they are:

- Assemble the team in a room with a flip chart, and no interruptions.

- Define the problem (as above) and write this up at the top of the flip chart. Encourage the team to quickly and spontaneously offer ideas to solve the problem. You may prefer to use sticky notes to write down and capture ideas rather than shouting them out.

- Be as concise as possible – do not elaborate/justify/defend/challenge; the objective here is to get as many ideas as possible.

- The team can either operate 'round robin' (taking it in turns to offer a suggestion) or randomly throw up ideas.

- The process should be fun, and everyone should be encouraged to throw up as many wacky ideas as possible – without debate!

When the ideas dry up, draw the brainstorm session to a conclusion. The next steps are:

- Check understanding; now is the time to explain any ideas that are not clear to the team.

- Incubate the ideas, over lunch... overnight. Reflect on the ideas – avoid rejecting them. See where you can build on ideas – and add new ones to the list. It is really important that people learn to build on each other's ideas, as many new ones are generated instantaneously, although it may take a whole team to put together a workable solution.

- Group similar ideas into common areas. You can then remove any duplication.

Once you have completed this phase, you can move to Stage 3 of the process: evaluation – it is time to select those ideas that are the strongest.

Tips on how to implement an improvement plan effectively

A service-improvement plan should be a living document that outlines the action you will take to improve your services, product, processes and people. One major retailer we work with ensures that each level of the organization has a plan. Each level's service-improvement plan is linked to the next – regional directors to area managers, and area managers to store managers for example – so that everyone is focusing on the same key improvement areas for the customer.

In order to create an effective service-improvement plan:

- Seek support from key stakeholders:

  Meet with the major stakeholders – for example your manager or service partners – and share with them the key themes of your findings around root-cause analysis of complaints. Discuss with them your initial analysis of the issue and the underlying cause. This will ensure that you have support and buy-in when developing your plan of action.

- Define clear action. This should include the following:
  - what needs to be done;
  - who needs to be involved;
  - when it needs to be completed;
  - timescales for milestones.

- Consider potential barriers:
  - What might the potential barriers be?
  - How much influence do you have over them?
  - Who else has influence?
  - What help might you need and from whom?
  - How motivated are you to achieve the improvement?

- Establish measures of success:
  - What will you have, that you don't have now, if the action is a success?
  - How do you define success? What are the measures?
  - What impact will this have on the customer?
  - Agree a review date for evaluating your progress with key stakeholders.

- Share results:

  Involving key stakeholders throughout the process is critical to success. They can help to remove the organizational barriers to being more customer focused, thereby supporting you in your work to better serve the customer.

- Publicize success:

  Don't forget to tell your customers what improvements you have made as a result!

Eastman Chemical root-cause analysis

At Eastman Chemical a root-cause analysis training course was developed and, in the first year alone, rolled out more than 300 people, representing every Eastman site worldwide. Additionally, 'complaint reduction through defect prevention' was made a corporate initiative. This was backed up by considerable management support and extensive measurement to allow progress to be monitored in terms of the number of complaints per million shipments. This measure was adopted by each site. The established goal was to cut the number of complaints by half over a three-year period through defect prevention.

Training covered the following key concepts:

- A structured logic tree process used to identify and verify hypotheses with data.
- It is important to go beyond human error and causes.
- The processes, systems, and the latent or organizational causes must be identified.
- Only by eliminating the real root causes can the probability of re-occurrence be reduced or eliminated.
- Investigation should not stop at the first 'root causes', but dig deeper to identify and eliminate the multiple causes.
- Problems are often the result of multiple rather than single causes.

Training sessions typically lasted between half a day and a full day. Another feature of the Eastman approach was to involve customers and suppliers in the root-cause analysis work. Three years on, Eastman has nearly halved the level of customer complaints.

Complaints as part of a wider customer feedback loop

Root-cause analysis is a method that helps companies to better understand what issues within the organization cause customers to complain, what can be done about them and how this will improve the company. Here is an example of one company that has adopted this approach:

LV= is the UK's largest friendly society (mutual) and sells a wide range of insurance from car insurance to life insurance, savings, travel, pet and home insurance. Both the general insurance and life insurance sectors are extremely competitive markets and LV= aims to give consistently high customer service throughout the customer journey from buying or taking out a new policy through to renewals, amendments to the policy or making a claim.

After discussing various options, it was decided that a monthly tracking survey would ensure constant customer focus, and data from complaints plus a monthly telephone survey would allow granular detail in terms of customer comments and trends. Each month LV= speaks to almost 1,000 customers to ensure accurate coverage across their varied types of customer. It also conducts root-cause analysis.

To ensure that results are fed back as quickly as possible, and to as many people as possible, the company designed a unique web report. This allows results and comments by segment to be easily accessed.

Quarterly workshops are arranged where senior managers discuss key findings, and action plans are quickly put into place. These may require actions from specific outside suppliers working on behalf of LV= or from specific teams within the company. Progress against these actions is then monitored in future surveys.

Other ways to generate ideas for service improvement

There are also lots of other practical ways to challenge existing ways of working:

- Assess the competition. Find out who your competitors are and how they operate. Use the internet and advertising sources to find out about their products and services, and how they deal with complaints.

- Study market or industry trends. Awareness of the climate in which your business is operating will help you to plan. You can find a lot of information about your industry on the internet. Business and trade magazines will also feature useful articles. There are often lots of industry reports about the complaint and customer-service arena.

- Involve your suppliers and other business partners. Pooling your resources with your third-party suppliers or other business partners will help you produce and develop creative ideas. Potential partnerships can also be developed through business networking opportunities.

- Benchmark your organization. Take the opportunity to find out about best practice in other organizations, both similar and different to your own. Attending conferences and networking events, and talking to other complaint-handling professionals can help trigger new ideas and improvements.

When Kent County Council wished to improve its services to its customers, it undertook an audit of what customer requirements were as well as looking at best practice in service excellence. It discovered that as well as home visits, web and telephone services, residents wanted convenient, physical access to frontline customer advisors from a wide range of public services, in a modern retail setting.

Kent County Council developed its service strategy by benchmarking itself to other retail outlets that offered services to the community. These included supermarket chain ASDA, which spends £4 million a year on a variety of social schemes. Each ASDA store allocates 80 hours staff time to community projects. Kent County Council also benchmarked itself against shopping centre Bluewater, which invests in waste management, has an ambulance base and a Learning Shop; the Discovery Channel Store in Washington DC, which creates a powerful social and educational experience; and pharmacy chain Boots, which offers hearing-care service advisors and baby- and childcare advisors.

Its service strategy led to the development of its Gateway retail stores where services include:

- information and self-help, including free internet, a service directory and a payment kiosk;
- advice and transactions, including bus passes, refuse, parking and licensing;
- cross-agency services, including council tax, benefits, planning, housing, a library, adult education and occupational therapy.

All its frontline staff are trained to deal with complaints.

Key learning points

- Root-cause analysis allows you to treat the causes of complaints, rather than dealing with the symptoms.

- Use your management information and techniques such as problem checklist, fishbone diagram and the five whys to arrive at a robust definition of the underlying causes of a complaint.

- Develop ongoing service-improvement plans and make sure you share successes with both employees and customers.

Creating an environment that promotes high performance

10

Complaint handling is not easy. Dealing with unhappy customers on a daily basis and championing the voice of the customer throughout the organization can be stressful. In some customer-relations departments, attrition can be particularly high and employee morale can be rock-bottom.

In this chapter I address how to create a positive environment in the workplace where people go above and beyond the call of duty to deliver excellent customer service. In particular, I look at the role of the manager in supporting and challenging the team members, providing coaching and feedback, and understanding what motivates their team.

The ideal complaint handler

The ideal complaint-handling team member is emotionally intelligent, demonstrates excellent communication skills and has the ability to empathize with unhappy customers. Good complaint handlers have a thorough knowledge of the organization's structure and processes and know where to go to retrieve relevant information about products and services. They are able to objectively assess all relevant factors about complaints from the point of view of both the customer and the company, to mediate in difficult situations and to identify root causes of complaints.

In summary, they have an enthusiasm for and a commitment to effective, fair and efficient complaints management and they are great team members too, going the extra mile for the customer. In summary, they are highly engaged employees. Do such people actually exist?

Loyalty and engagement

Employee loyalty cannot be taken for granted: various surveys have shown that typically over half an organization's employees are expecting to leave voluntarily within two years. We should not see this as acceptable, because what is lost with every person who leaves is tacit knowledge about the customer. Service levels are bound to suffer as new employees are trained up and extra cover and training is taken into account. The open and hidden costs of attrition include:

- reduction in operational efficiency and customer-service levels once the individual has decided to leave;
- loss of knowledge about the customer base that the leaver has acquired;
- the costs of recruitment and selection – recruitment agency costs, and the HR department's, managers' and team leaders' time;
- costs of induction – initial training and development: individuals', managers', team leaders' and HR department's time;
- costs of ongoing training – both for courses and one-to-one coaching;
- reduction in operational efficiency and customer-service levels while the individual is trained to agreed standards, including the impact on existing team members;
- costs of training and development for another team member to bring them to team leader standard.

A survey in the United States estimated customers had suffered in 40 per cent of organizations as a result of staff leaving.

An example of the damaging effects of attrition can be illustrated by Chris, a talented customer-service representative in a service company we know well. She had a cheerful manner and a strong rapport with customers, and was very knowledgeable when dealing with complaints. She had good team leader potential yet after two years she was complaining that her managers didn't respect her and she wasn't treated fairly. She became reluctant to take on extra work and began to contribute to a sour climate in her team, which leaked out to the customers. She eventually left to go to a competitor. Management had tried to save her. 'No,' she said: the last-minute offers of promotion were too vague and the salary promises insufficient. Where, her manager asked us, had he gone wrong? The company had lost someone that was going to take a lot to replace in a small team of specialist complaint handlers.

While most companies proclaim the importance of their staff in delivering service to the customer, many employees who deal with the customers experience a mismatch between words and deeds. As a consequence, they do not feel engaged with the company.

Engagement can be summed up by how positively the employee:

- thinks about the organization;
- feels about the organization;
- is proactive in relation to achieving organizational goals for customers;
- relates to colleagues and other stakeholders.

This can be seen in the degree to which they perform their role in a positive and proactive manner.

Often employees do not get sufficient encouragement to continue to stay and commit themselves fully, and much of this can be traced back to the way they are managed. Yet there is a proven link to retention between internal service quality, employee satisfaction and positive customer relationships.

Research studies find that positive employee attitudes led to an increase of over a third in customer satisfaction, with higher productivity and profits. The service profit chain, developed by Earl Sasser from work undertaken at Sears, also demonstrates this link. This is discussed in the next few sections.

Concentrate on your people first

A good example of a company that pays attention to employees' needs with the customer in mind is financial services group first direct. It could have followed the call centre norm and treated employees as dispensable fodder. Instead, it consciously created a mission of a 'great place to work' and thought carefully about the needs of its employees. Since 80 per cent are women, often working in a 24-hour environment, it paid extra attention to their needs for personal security, for example with controlled parking spaces, and also provided a large crèche facility. To give employees and customers the best possible experience, new employees are given a thorough five-week induction, accredited training, and rewards for successful performance. Managers carry out twice-yearly opinion surveys among employees – and act on the results.

First direct has a well-thought-out retention strategy, involving:

- recruitment – selecting the right people who will give the customer the right experience and who are likely to stay;
- resource deployment – so the employee isn't over-stretched and can deliver to the customer;
- competency definition – clarity of role;
- development using accreditations – sound development with motivational stages;
- benchmarking – to pinpoint success;
- performance management – spotting issues early and managing progress supportively;
- career management – nurturing of talent;
- reward and recognition – encouraging the right things.

Underpinning all of this is clear leadership, with pervading customer and employee-orientated values.

Healthcare organization BUPA is another organization that knows that the success of its increased customer-focused efforts rest on careful attention to its employees. In the words of BUPA's Catrin Weston: 'Pursuing the goal of improving staff satisfaction, loyalty and commitment was not just a liberal/good employer thing to do. It had real, tangible results for our customers and for BUPA's profitability.'

How engaged are your work colleagues?

One way of describing the level of engagement among employees is to gauge their enthusiasm and energy level and the degree of positivity that they display at work. Think about people in your place of work as I describe the following model of engagement.

The model has two dimensions:

- the employees – attitude towards the customer, their colleagues and the organization, be it positive or negative;
- their enthusiasm and drive towards activity, be it positive and active or negative and inactive.

The degree to which people demonstrate a positive attitude and their type and levels of activity can be translated into likely engagement patterns. Figure 10.1 illustrates simple behavioural patterns that can be seen in regard to engagement.

FIGURE 10.1 Engagement levels

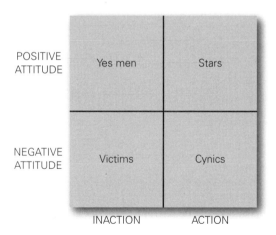

Stars: Have a positive attitude to change and are action orientated. They have high energy and enthusiasm, and are willing to go the extra mile. They are realistic about obstacles they encounter and how to overcome these.

Stars are fully engaged with the organization. Their behaviour is characterized by:

- giving discretionary effort to serve the customer;
- seeing the silver lining hidden beneath the dark clouds;
- viewing change as challenge and opportunity;
- treating life as a continuous learning experience;
- expanding their personal comfort zone.

Stars tend to:

- feel comfortable with the need for change;
- be open to possibilities and ideas;
- be optimistic about the long-term future;
- like to be challenged and stretched;
- be realists, not afraid of short-term mistakes or setbacks.

Cynics: Display a negative attitude and high levels of activity. This group are actively disengaged. They have a lot of energy and can be very vocal but what they focus on is the negative – what is not working in the organization. They are keen to disassociate themselves from the organization and tell others why change won't work.

Cynic behaviour is characterized by:

- always seeing the negatives;
- criticizing ideas and solutions;
- expressing frustration;
- focusing on the past: 'We tried this five years ago...';
- arguing against change;
- being oblivious to the consequences of their negativity;
- bringing the other people such as 'victims' and the 'yes men' round to their perspective.

Cynics feel:

- 'right' and angry at the world for ignoring them;
- frustrated when there is confusion and 'whinging';

- not listened to, excluded, constrained;
- overtly confident in their own ability;
- rebellious, determined to block change they do not own;
- unsympathetic to the stress felt by others.

Yes men: This group of people is characterized as neither actively engaged nor disengaged. They are the 'coasters', prepared to drift along, saying the right things but following things through with energy, passion or action.

Yes men are characterized by behaviour that is about:

- avoiding taking risks;
- keeping a low profile;
- trying to ride things out without drawing attention to themselves;
- acknowledging good ideas but being reluctant to change themselves.

Although yes men may be positive about what is happening in an organization, they are reluctant to get involved. They feel threatened when too exposed and are comfortable to watch from the sidelines.

Victims: Can be described as having a negative attitude and lacking drive. This inactivity coupled with their negative approach towards new ideas leads to inertia. Although less vocal than cynics, they still are disengaged from the organization, everything is 'done to them', they do not take an active part in organizational life. However, unlike cynics they lack the energy or drive to vocalise this.

Victims react by:

- not confronting issues;
- retreating into 'safety' – burying their heads in the sand;
- avoiding risk, doing the minimum;
- avoiding thinking about what might happen.

Victims may feel unhappy and/or depressed, overwhelmed by work, powerless and fearful of mistakes but their lack of confidence means that they do not actively seek to find other employment or to improve their current working life.

FIGURE 10.2 Characteristic phrases

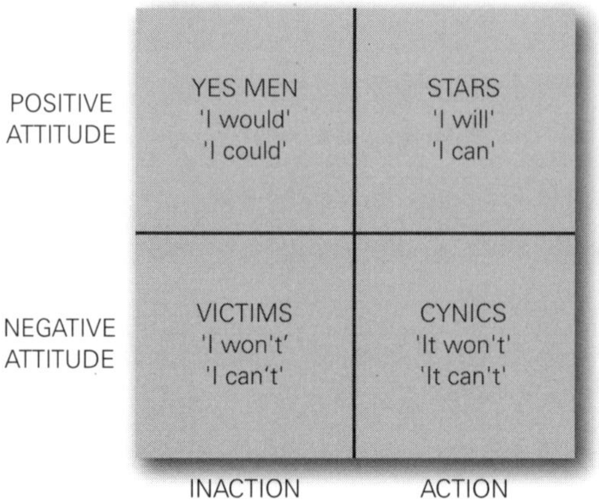

	INACTION	ACTION
POSITIVE ATTITUDE	YES MEN 'I would' 'I could'	STARS 'I will' 'I can'
NEGATIVE ATTITUDE	VICTIMS 'I won't' 'I can't'	CYNICS 'It won't' 'It can't'

Figure 10.2 shows the words that each type may characteristically use when dealing with a customer who complains.

So how do you make more people in your team into stars?

A lot of research has been done on the key influencers of engagement in a service environment. People have looked at influencers such as the layout of the workplace, pay and benefits, and feeling part of a team. However, it is generally accepted that the biggest influence on how much extra effort people want to put into their job is their direct line manager.

People join an organization and leave a manager

As my example of Chris shows earlier, when people are disengaged, it is often because they are not happy with their manager. An effective manager creates a work climate where individuals feel able to give of their best, to learn and develop to their full potential. Studies show that when people leave an organization to go elsewhere it is often because of the relationship they have with their direct line manager or supervisor. A typical complaint is that the manager did not appreciate them and did nothing but criticize them, or that the manager did not stretch them enough or give them the opportunity to shine.

Many managers would feel very uncomfortable if they heard their staff's honest responses to these key questions:

- Am I rewarded for going the extra mile for the customer?
- Is there investment in training and developing me?
- Are my ideas listened to?
- Does the company allow me the flexibility and give me authority to solve customer issues?
- Do managers hold me in high esteem?

An important way managers can create a positive work environment is by reinforcing helpful behaviour in individuals and challenging less effective behaviour. Yet all too often managers fail to provide effective feedback to individuals in their team, or if they do they fail to balance the amount of supportive and challenging feedback that they give. Managers at retailer John Lewis are encouraged to use the formula of three to one: catch people getting it right three times more often than you catch them getting it wrong and you will get the best out of people.

Balancing support and challenge

Experience of working with a wide number of managers across many industry sectors shows that those who are most successful demonstrate an appropriate mixture of supportive, reinforcing behaviours and challenging, questioning behaviours, according to the needs of the staff member with whom they are dealing.

Supportive behaviours include:

- offering positive feedback;
- listening;
- empathizing;
- providing assistance, guidance and backup for others;
- helping with resources;
- giving their own time and effort.

Challenging behaviours are:

- offering formative feedback;
- pushing others to do better by making requests and setting targets;
- asking them to rethink their actions and decisions by questioning and offering alternatives;
- confronting issues assertively.

The range of styles is shown in Figure 10.3.

FIGURE 10.3 Support and challenge

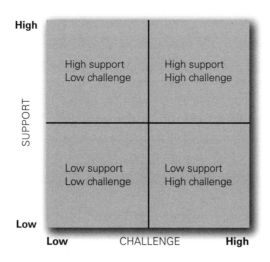

When a manager uses a highly challenging but unsupportive style, the environment that is created is often stressful and task focused. This style of leadership can breed 'cynics' who have disengaged from the organization and want to do their own thing.

A manager who is highly supportive but unchallenging creates a 'cosy' environment, where the emphasis is on maintaining relationships but not necessarily getting things done. Typically this makes for a cosy team but people drift and become 'yes men', doing anything for an easy life.

An environment of low challenge and low support can lead to apathy and low morale. People become disempowered and have low self-esteem. They act as and become 'victims'.

FIGURE 10.4 The impact of the different styles on team members

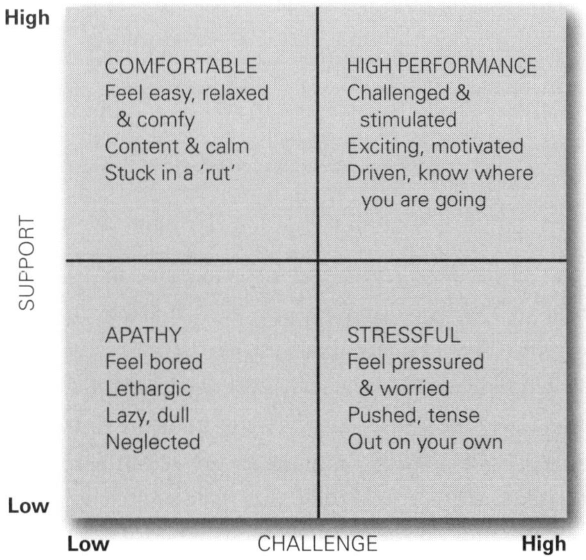

In environments where there is an inappropriate balance of the two styles, the long-term effect on team members of working can be a mixture of unhelpful behaviours; the right balance leads to people feeling stretched and supported, comfortable with the need for change, open to possibilities and ideas (Figure 10.4).

High challenge and high support brings about high performance. This in turn will lead to high levels of customer service. You will have lots of 'stars' in your team if you adopt this balance.

Providing regular feedback

Creating a high-performance culture is underpinned by the ability to give effective feedback. As the purpose of feedback is to improve performance and to keep people on track, providing feedback on performance should be a regular part of a manager's role. So why do many managers neglect this important skill or leave it to the annual performance review?

Some people hold back from giving motivational feedback because they think that compliments are inappropriate, because staff are only doing what they are paid to do. Sometimes people don't give praise and recognition because:

- They feel too embarrassed.
- They believe that the person receiving the feedback may relax and take it easy.
- They believe that the person receiving the feedback may be suspicious of their motives.
- They think that the feedback may be misinterpreted as a ploy to fish for compliments in return.
- They don't like receiving motivational feedback themselves.

Some managers hold back from giving developmental feedback because they worry that they might upset the receiver, they are concerned that the receiver may reject them or the feedback. Others are concerned that the person might retaliate with developmental feedback about the manager. They are worried that the discussion may end in a confrontation that would be difficult to resolve and might damage future relationships. Or they may think that the issue is too trivial, and that feedback would be better kept in reserve for something more substantial. Maybe they don't like receiving developmental feedback themselves.

Tips on giving feedback

Fundamental to being able to give effective feedback is the belief that feedback is a helpful, healthy and positive communication between two people. The purpose of feedback is to maintain and improve performance – it therefore should have both a positive intention and impact. Consequently it is vital that the whole feedback process, whether giving motivational feedback, (what has gone well) or developmental feedback (where the individual can improve) is conducted in a positive and constructive way.

Imagine you have to give feedback to someone in your team who has handled a complaint well, or someone who has not done a good job. Here are ten tips for giving effective feedback to complaint handlers.

When you have to give feedback about how someone handled a complaint:

1 Prioritize your feedback – don't overload the receiver with too much feedback as this is difficult to take in.

2 Provide feedback on observed behaviour – what the individual has said or done; don't make subjective judgements.

3 Be specific – use examples, don't make generalizations.

4 Give motivational feedback before formative. It is better not to start on a negative when you have a positive to offer too.

5 Do separate motivational from developmental feedback. Do not link the two with the words 'but' or 'however' as this negates what has gone before.

6 Be clear about what the individual did well and what they could do to improve. Don't use a positive, negative, positive sandwich such as saying: 'The first part of your presentation was well structured, but the second part was not as clear. Although overall you did really well,' as this leaves the individual with the impression that everything is OK when it is not!

7 Ask questions when giving feedback – don't make the conversation one-sided, ask the individual what they think they did well, where they think they can improve.

8 Time your feedback – say it while it is fresh. Don't wait till a long time after the event.

9 Own the feedback – don't feed back on behaviour that you have not observed but that has been reported to you by someone else.

10 Have a positive intention when you give feedback. Don't use feedback to 'get at someone'; the purpose of feedback is to help the individual.

Courageous conversations

Undoubtedly there will be occasions when you have to hold a difficult or 'courageous' conversation with a team member. You may think: 'Why should I have a difficult conversation at all?' However, delaying until the 'right time' comes along usually results in the problem not being dealt with. The situation will usually not go away and a problem will not usually resolve itself. For example, you may hear someone being aggressive to a customer on the telephone. Not dealing with it can lead to new complications, making it difficult to deal with.

So how do you go about managing a difficult conversation? Once you have decided to address the issue by having a conversation with the individual, you need to prepare what to say. Think about what the ideal outcome of the conversation would be. Investigate the issue to be able to provide evidence of the message you are imparting and prepare any documentation you might need. Practise what you are going to say. This will help you gain confidence. It's helpful to ask someone you trust for some feedback beforehand about how you come across.

When you are talking to the person, state the issues clearly. Don't beat around the bush. Provide specific examples and evidence to avoid misunderstandings. Aim to put the message across in a way that is constructive and positive.

Don't do all the talking! Asking questions will help gather useful information about the issue. Do listen and give the other person plenty of time to respond. It is important that you find out more about the matter from the other person's perspective. Find out what they believe is the best way to resolve the issue. Once you've established this, seek to jointly agree a way forward. Once you have agreed a plan of action, remember to agree when you will review this.

Dealing with reactions to feedback

Ideally people should be receptive to feedback and see it as helpful. When people receive feedback, they have a choice whether to accept what they are told or not. However in order to ensure that they understand the feedback, they need to listen and avoid rejecting what has been said, arguing or being defensive. In reality a wide variety of reactions occur. People may:

- Deny what has happened. This reaction often accompanies the initial shock of feedback.
- Show emotion. Be upset, angry or go quiet as the message sinks in.
- Justify their actions and find excuses for their behaviour.

To help your feedback be more effective when someone denies what you are saying, reiterate the facts. Explain what you saw or heard. If the team member shows emotion, listen actively and you could empathize with his or her situation. If the discussion gets very heated, you may need to postpone any further discussion until later when the team member is more receptive. If the person to whom you are giving the feedback makes excuses, discuss the standards that are expected. Encourage them to take ownership by asking them what they could do differently to prevent the situation happening again.

Feedback can help a manager maintain and improve their team members' performance and, when well delivered, can play an important part in creating a high-performance culture. Our experience is that managers do benefit from receiving training and coaching in effective feedback skills. However, like any skill, unless it is practised regularly it can become difficult to apply. Managers need to be aware of people's reactions to feedback and deal with them appropriately in order to support change.

Coaching to improve performance

One technique that successful managers use to get the best from their team is coaching. Coaching is a forward-focused and goal-orientated tool that can help you improve the performance of individuals on your team. In addition it can help you resolve issues you may face with colleagues, key stakeholders or even your boss. By adopting a coaching approach, you are more likely to achieve high levels of both employee engagement and customer satisfaction.

What is coaching?

There are various definitions of coaching:

- an ongoing professional relationship that helps people achieve extraordinary results;
- helping people to unlock their potential;
- the process of accelerating an individual's progress to achieving personal and organizational goals;
- the partnership between a manager and an individual, whereby the manager helps the individual to learn.

The purpose of coaching is to help individuals define desired outcomes, to create awareness of the options open to them in achieving their desired outcomes and to help them take responsibility for developing appropriate strategies and actions to achieve them.

Coaching versus training

Coaching is different from training, which involves teaching something, usually a skill. The coaching process assumes that the coachees have the ability to find the resources they need to achieve their goal. Coaching is about helping people to learn, rather than teaching them.

What are the benefits of coaching?

Coaching is a proven way of improving performance in a business setting. It is a technique that all managers will find invaluable. One of the benefits of coaching is that it can be applied to many settings and undertaken in as short a time as 15 minutes. *Fortune* magazine undertook a survey in 2006 about the benefits to companies that encouraged coaching. Its research found that coaching resulted in increases in:

- productivity (reported by 53 per cent of respondents);
- quality (48 per cent);
- organizational strength (48 per cent);
- customer service (39 per cent).

Respondents also reported benefits in the following areas:

- reducing customer complaints (34 per cent);
- retaining executives who received coaching (32 per cent);
- cost reductions (23 per cent);
- bottom-line profitability (22 per cent).

Coaching and feedback sits at the heart of the performance-management cycle. It should be an ongoing and regular event.

Organizations such as Sears in the United States have used coaching as part of their performance-management process on an ongoing basis. In an article in the *Harvard Business Review*, authors Rucci, Kim and Quinn discuss how coaching contributed to the turnaround of Sears: 'In their "turnaround" effort, the company's mission was to have Sears be a "compelling place to work, a compelling place to shop, and compelling place to invest".'

They set up rigorous measurements for (among other things) employee attitude and satisfaction. One of their primary questions was 'How does the way you are treated by those who supervise you influence your overall attitude about your job?' Their statistics showed that as the quality of management improved, so did employee attitudes, and then customer satisfaction. The numbers showed that 'a five-point improvement in employee attitudes will drive a 1.3 point improvement in customer satisfaction, which in turn will drive a 0.5 per cent improvement in revenue growth.'

In a billion-dollar company, a 0.5 per cent increase in revenue is substantial. Sears learned that when their managers fully value and develop their employees (ie, use the coaching approach), they could confidently predict future revenue growth in a particular district. When employee satisfaction increased by 5 per cent, revenue growth in a particular store increased by 5.5 per cent.

GROW model of coaching

The GROW model of coaching, developed by Sir John Whitmore, uses a series of open questions to help the individual to raise awareness and increase responsibility and ownership. GROW is a mnemonic that stands for Goal, Reality, Options and Will or Way forward.

The key to using this sequence effectively is to be flexible as a coach; for example you may reach the second or third stage then find a need to backtrack and redefine the goal. The flexible coach will use the guide in a dynamic way to match the needs of the coachee.

You will also notice that an important stage in the process is Reality: where the coachee is now. Whitmore, like Gallwey before him, found that in conversations people typically talk about the past, discuss their goal going forward and then move straight to the future. Gallwey found that in encouraging coachees to focus on what is happening now, he enabled them to look at their performance from a different perspective. This brought them insights and harnessed their intuition, which allowed them to generate options and actions for the future.

Below we outline the key stages of the GROW process.

Goal Ask the coachee to describe the desired goal or outcome precisely in positive terms.

Make this sensory specific evidence – what will they see, hear, feel when this is achieved?

Make the goal SMART – Specific, Measurable, Achievable, Realistic, Timebound.

Reality Ask the coachee to describe what is the reality or current situation.

Ask them how they currently perceive their performance in relation to their objective.

Ask the coachee if it helps to give themselves a benchmark – for example to rate themselves on a 1 to 10 scale in terms of where they are now and where they want to be.

Options Ask the coachee to explore the situation or problem and to outline options for a solution. Encourage them not to have 'the solution' instantly.

Encourage the coachee to generate as many ideas for improvement as possible.

Ask them if there was a way for them to reach their objective, what it would be.

Will/Way forward Ask coachees to select idea/s they will put into practice.

Ask them what they will do. When? How?

Discuss who else they need to involve in the actions and what resources are needed.

Discuss any barriers to achieving the actions and how these can be overcome.

By adopting this enabling coaching approach, managers encourage much more responsibility and accountability in their team members.

Developing a strategy for engagement

Coaching is one important way of engaging employees. In promoting engagement and retention practices, watch out for some common pitfalls that undermine effectiveness:

- failure to regularly monitor signals;
- the assumption that one approach fits everyone;
- the belief that it's all down to money;
- saying 'it's not my problem'.

Managers who are about improving engagement need to sit down together and honestly appraise where the organization is now in terms of retention and where it needs to be.

A starting point is to look at what matters to the organization to ensure its service success, and also the roles that particularly support this. You probably already have a lot of data from employee turnover figures, employee surveys, focus groups, exit interviews and opportunities for employees to 'talk back' to managers in a candid way. Travel company Airtours solicited staff views on the actions that affected customers, what could be improved and how people felt about the company. This was based on the notion that the best way to develop a quality service was to enhance employees' abilities to improve the company's services. Some companies are tapping into official and unofficial bulletin-board websites where employees vent their feelings.

Do not rely on pay and conditions alone as the basis of a retention strategy

Many organizations depend on motivating employees to stay via incentives such as pay and good working conditions. Recent surveys of why call centre staff defect to other companies indicate that pay is a major factor. Further research reveals that employees are more likely to move on if they believe that they are not receiving a fair deal. Yet relying on external hygiene factors such as pay and conditions is only a temporary motivator. Yes, it is important to get these right, but even when people consider they are rewarded fairly, they may not necessarily stay with the organization.

To foster long-term, sustained engagement and motivation, recent thought is that organizations must inspire employees to draw their motivation from within rather than rely on external factors such as pay. In his book *SuperMotivation*, the American management guru Dean Spitzer has identified eight fundamental needs that motivate employees in the long term and that are shared to varying degrees by us all. These are:

- *The need for activity*. People want to be active and involved. In our personal lives most people avoid boredom and monotony. Yet at work employees are expected to accept boring, repetitious, monotonous jobs with little autonomy.
- *The need for ownership*. Owning things makes people feel better about themselves. 'Psychological' ownership is even more important than 'physical' ownership. Employees want to psychologically own their work. They want to control input into their work and to feel responsible for their jobs.

- *The need for power.* People want to control their destiny. They don't want to feel powerless in the face of external forces shaping their lives. With fewer top-down control organizations, more and more employees are demanding their freedom back.

- *The need for affiliation.* People are social creatures. They like to interact and socialize with one another, although the degree of sociability will vary. Social support and helping relationships are among the many benefits provided by work.

- *The need for competence.* This is the core of self-esteem. People welcome opportunities to feel more competent. Work can provide these opportunities.

- *The need for achievement.* It is important for us to succeed at something. Under the right conditions, employees will be willing to work hard and overcome obstacles to achieve a goal.

- *The need for recognition.* People want to feel appreciated by others and be positively recognized for their efforts. Recognition is a powerful force that can unleash energy and motivation.

- *The need for meaning.* People want a reason for doing something. They want reassurance that their efforts, however small, are making a difference.

Use the questionnaire at the end of this chapter with your team to see what their motivators are and how you can get the best from them.

Adopt a tailored approach

Make sure you adopt a targeted approach when considering how you can engage your staff to deliver excellent service. For example, research shows younger groups emphasize development and career advancement, whilst older groups particularly value benefits such as pensions. Hold a focus group or use employee survey data to analyse the degree of satisfaction with:

- pay and benefits;
- degree of ownership and challenge in the job;
- development – now and for the future;

- performance management;
- the culture of your firm.

An employee survey in a software company on recognition methods fed back the following priority: 'First, say thank you more often.' Employees need to feel their contribution is valued, yet many service departments feel they are in a backwater in their companies. A US survey found that the most significant motivator that employees receive is a personal thank you or a handwritten note from their manager.

Key learning points

- Be warned against complacency when it comes to engaging team members. It is too easy to be satisfied with answers that suggest that high attrition is the norm in customer service.

- By getting the balance right between the support you give team members and the degree of challenge, you can create a climate of high performance.

- Providing regular feedback – both motivational and developmental – and ongoing coaching is an essential way to reinforce positive behaviours in complaint handlers and to raise the bar.

What are your team members' motivators?

You can use this questionnaire to see what motivates your team members – and you can also use it yourself!

Look at the list below and score each statement on a scale of 1 (not very important to me) to 10 (very important indeed to me):

		Your score
1.	Having fun at work	
2.	Feeling you have a stake in the organization's success	
3.	Feeling in control of your own destiny	
4.	Having opportunities to socialize	
5.	Feeling competent at your job	
6.	Succeeding at your work	
7.	Receiving encouragement	
8.	Being shown the significance of your work	
9.	Being asked for your input	
10.	Being able to make choices at work	
11.	Being given responsibility for your work	
12.	Working in a team with a powerful identity	
13.	Using your hidden strengths	
14.	Being allowed to set goals for yourself	
15.	Being shown appreciation	
16.	Knowing that what you do makes a difference	
17.	Having variety at work	
18.	Owning the work you do	
19.	Being given leadership opportunities	
20.	Being a valued member of a team	
21.	Being given learning opportunities	
22.	Being encouraged to improve	
23.	Being recognized for your effort	
24.	Being able to relate your objectives to the bigger picture	
25.	Feeling active and involved	

	Your score
26. Feeling responsible for what you do	_____
27. Feeling empowered to make decisions	_____
28. Feeling you belong	_____
29. Being able to learn through mistakes	_____
30. Being challenged to stretch your limits	_____
31. Feeling rewarded for success	_____
32. Having meaning from your job	_____

Transfer your scores to the grid below. Then add the total of each category working across the page, eg for Category A, total the sum of your scores for statements 1, 9, 17 and 25.

Statement number:	Statement number:	Statement number:	Statement number:	Category total
1	9	17	25	A
2	10	18	26	B
3	11	19	27	C
4	12	20	28	D
5	13	21	29	E
6	14	22	30	F
7	15	23	31	G
8	16	24	32	H

Now identify the two categories in which you score the highest.

Interpreting your scores

This questionnaire is designed to identify the work conditions that help you and your team feel motivated. It works on the principle that motivation comes from within. Other people cannot motivate us. However, they can contribute to a motivating environment by satisfying one of the following needs that we may have. Your two highest scores will relate to one of the following categories:

Category A: Activity	being active and involved at work
Category B: Ownership	being able to own your work
Category C: Power	being empowered, taking control
Category D: Belonging	feeling part of a group
Category E: Competency	feeling able to use and develop your skills
Category F: Achievement	feeling that goals are reached
Category G: Recognition	being recognized for effort and success
Category H: Meaning	feeling that what you do has significance

Helping others feel motivated

Once you know what the motivators are for your team members, consider what you can do to satisfy them. Here are some suggestions, although you may find it helpful to have a one-to-one discussion with individual team members to help establish their thoughts and feelings.

Remember, what motivates you may not be necessarily the same as your team, so do not treat everyone as if they were you!

Desire for activity

Make work more active.
Build fun into work.
Ask for people's input.
Add variety to work.

Desire for ownership

Give people a stake in the firm's success.
Let people make choices more often.

Desire for power

Give people responsibility for their work.
Provide leadership opportunities.

Desire for affiliation

Offer opportunities to socialize.
Create a powerful team identity.

Desire for competence

Use people's hidden strengths.
Provide learning opportunities.
Tolerate mistakes.

Desire for achievement

Provide objective performance measures.
Let people set goals for themselves.
Encourage team members to improve.
Challenge people to stretch their limits.

Desire for recognition

Provide encouragement.
Show your appreciation.

Desire for meaning

Show people the significance of their work.

Complaint handling and culture change

11

Complaint handling is only one aspect of the customer journey, yet as we have seen it is a critical one. Complaint handling is a very good indicator of the culture of an organization as it demonstrates to what extent organizations are treating customers fairly. In this last chapter I look at the characteristics of excellent service organizations and I share best practice in terms of complaint management. I hope that the examples will inspire you!

Customer service and culture change

A recent study undertaken by the Institute of Customer Service found that those organizations with an excellent reputation in their customers' eyes had a 72 per cent higher level of profit per employee on a like-for-like basis compared with those companies with a poor reputation. They also produced a higher net margin and a higher return on total assets.

It is many businesses' ambition to create a culture where individuals want to and do provide an excellent service. Yet our research shows that only a few organizations truly succeed in this aim. Creating a customer-centric business is a long-term process that requires persistence and commitment. It is not enough to provide training in customer care skills to staff. A customer-service ethic needs to be present in every aspect of how the organization does its business.

FIGURE 11.1 Eight characteristics of excellent service organizations

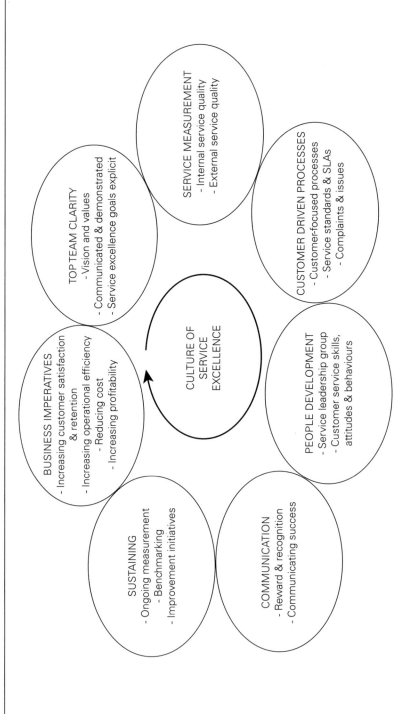

Changing a culture is a long process; it can take between three and five years. Learning from complaints can help effect change in the organization but in reality it is just one aspect of how an organization can become customer-focused.

Community pharmacy group Lloyds Pharmacy has been rated one of the top five organizations in the UK for delivering excellent service. Government legislation has expanded the community pharmacist role; pharmacists in the UK can now offer a wider range of services such as diabetes and cholesterol control, medicine usage review and smoking cessation sessions. At the same time the marketplace has been opened up to greater competition in the form of supermarkets. This has been a big change for the 2,500 pharmacy outlets in the Lloyds group, which employs over 17,000 staff. It has required a clear focus on the customer, the community and the NHS partners with whom the group works.

In order to engage everyone in the change, the business created a strong vision of the future and translated the transformation story into six easy pictures that helped people understand what they were being asked to do and why. The business set up a change-management team to help ensure the continuity of messaging. It particularly engaged the middle-management level in the changes that were taking place and exploring ways they could work more closely alongside GPs and hospitals. In addition the company has introduced a training programme called Best Care for all staff, where staff consider every possible way that they can help customers. The company recognizes that it is only half-way on the change journey but is already seeing an increase in positive customer feedback.

Figure 11.1 shows what needs to be in place to create a climate of excellent service.

Eight characteristics of excellent service organizations

Research we have conducted in my consultancy shows that highly effective customer-service organizations have eight distinctive characteristics. I have related these characteristics to examples around complaint handling.

1. Customer satisfaction and retention are key business imperatives

Those companies that are truly customer-focused ensure that everyone knows that ensuring customers are satisfied and keeping customers loyal is fundamental to the health of the business. In order to sustain long-term growth this is as important (if not more so) as improving margins and reducing costs.

Here are some examples so you can see how this translates into complaint management:

US up-market department store Nordstrom is well-known for its successful sales culture and high levels of customer service. All employees work on a commission basis with a minimum salary. The most successful sales assistants are those who provide the best service and earn the highest take-home pay.

One of the best-known examples of service excellence is thought to be what happened at the Nordstrom's Anchorage store soon after its purchase from Northern Commercial Company. A customer, unaware that the store had changed hands, returned a set of tyres. Although Nordstrom had never sold tyres since opening, it accepted that it was not the customer's fault that the store had changed hands, and the return was accepted. Many Nordstrom customers will attest that Nordstrom will refund items purchased at any time from Nordstrom stores.

All new employees are given a copy of Nordstrom's Employee Philosophy:

Welcome to Nordstrom

We're glad to have you with our Company. Our number one goal is to provide outstanding customer service. Set both your personal and professional goals high. We have great confidence in your ability to achieve them.

Nordstrom Rules: Rule #1: Use good judgment in all situations. There will be no additional rules.

Please feel free to ask your department manager, store manager, or division general manager any question at any time.

Another example is food retailer, ASDA. There the best colleagues work on the customer-service desk. The Customer Care Manager is responsible for the customers from the time they enter the car park until they leave the store.

In settling complaints it really does not matter what the complaint costs – keeping the customer is the focus. An incident-management group is pulled together within half an hour of a problem being identified and resolution is quickly devised and communicated to the other stores. Rebuilding the relationship after a complaint is very simple, given one key condition: everyone in the business has to 'get it' – everyone must clearly understand what they are expected to do.

At Singapore telecoms company Singtel, the guiding principle around complaint handling is: 'give the customer the benefit of the doubt'. The first point of contact is responsible for receiving and resolving the complaint and for doing whatever it takes to rebuild the customer's trust.

2. There is clarity and support at the top for delivering an excellent customer experience

Leaders have a responsibility for communicating the importance of customer care to all employees. It is helpful for leaders in a business to share with everyone their vision for the future of the company and the values that are important for everyone to demonstrate. If, however, leaders say one thing and do another, the customer-service message is likely to become diluted. Employees can soon become cynical if they see their leaders' words as empty. If leaders are not passionate about service, it is likely that their employees will not be either.

Here are some examples of companies where senior managers actively encourage effective complaint management through positive role modelling.

WPA Health Insurance has a main board director with the title Director of Best Practice whose responsibilities include complaints management. Management commitment is also demonstrated by offering every customer who complains a personal visit anywhere in the UK from a senior manager. In addition to demonstrating senior management commitment to staff and customers, these visits also give managers the opportunity to learn firsthand why the organization failed its customers. They hear the unfiltered 'voice of the customer'.

At financial services company first direct, the CEO is located alongside call centre agents, with his desk in the corner of the Leeds call centre. As well as making himself available for staff members who feel there is an issue to be resolved, he also takes calls directly from customers if they or the call centre agent thinks that is appropriate.

At Network Rail, in order to gain customer insight at the point of service delivery, senior managers set up and work at booths in stations during peak commuting times, allowing customers to provide direct feedback. This not only makes it easy for customers to complain when grievances are fresh in their mind, but also allows managers to engage in conversation with the customer, to better understand the problem from the customer's perspective, to investigate the root cause of the problem and obtain the customer's views on potential solutions. Although this is a difficult task for senior management (angry commuters being a somewhat hostile audience) it has proven a highly effective way to understand what matters most to customers and allow them to express grievances. It also sends a message to customers and staff that management are interested in the customer experience and complaints.

3. Customer measurement

Truly customer-focused organizations listen to the voice of the customer. They regularly measure customer satisfaction and disseminate the results of the feedback to their employees. They track customer satisfaction both externally and internally. The quality of the service that internal departments provide to each other is often indicative of the quality of external customer service.

Asking for feedback from customers within the organization is important. Like external customer measurement, internal measurement can take place via face-to-face interviews, customer focus groups, e-mail, or postal and telephone questionnaires. Many organizations also conduct employee attitude surveys to gauge the level of engagement of their employees. This is a useful way of identifying and implementing areas for improvement. Here are examples of five companies who are actively measuring their customer service and complaints activity.

Airline Emirates' service recovery strategy is based on the proactive identification of actual or potential service failures. This includes:

- inspectors from the service audit team regularly assessing Emirates' actual customer experience, both on the ground and in the air;
- conducting mystery shopping surveys and in-flight passenger surveys.

The specific Customer Affairs and Service Audit Department role is:

- to engage customers who are dissatisfied;
- to win back lost goodwill and income;
- to use customer feedback and service audit experiences to identify where failure is occurring or is likely to occur and drive improvement;
- to contribute to company revenue and profit.

Recognizing the benefits of rapid service recovery at the front line, management are seeking ways to give more empowerment to customer-facing staff.

Logistics company FedEx monitors performance on 12 Service Quality Indicators (SQI) in order to direct improvement efforts. It uses the SQI to guide management's and employees' efforts. The 12 key components of SQI have been determined through extensive customer research and represent the most important service and operating dimensions correlating with customer satisfaction. Some of these include damaged packages, lost packages, missed pickups, aircraft delays and complaints.

In order to assess levels of customer satisfaction after a complaint has been closed, First Chicago Bank conducts telephone interviews. These are normally conducted by employees from a range of functional departments across the organization, such as HR, finance, sales and quality assurance. Because staff from a range of departments participate, people across the bank become more aware of customer issues, the effort and cooperation needed to resolve them, and how to prevent them.

A key output from this activity is that the interviewer will also prepare a 'Follow-up Activator', which is a recommendation of any actions that the bank should take to ensure the satisfaction of the customer, based upon the customer's comments during the interview. Supporting the initiative is a senior vice president who is in charge of the process. The senior vice president has also been trained and certified and personally gets involved in the survey process.

To ensure complaints reach a stage where both the organization and customer agree it is closed satisfactorily, building society Norwich and Peterborough has established a Members Panel. This panel, which is made up entirely of its customers (members), will hear appeals from any customer (member) who is not happy with the resolution offered for a complaint. Management is committed to abiding by the panel's decision, even if the panel decides the outcome offered is not satisfactory and must be improved or changed.

In addition the CEO is sent a sample of complaints each week and will personally contact the customer to gain a better understanding of customer issues and to resolve the complaint.

American Express (Amex) has processes and systems in place that track customer behaviour after a complaint has officially been closed. This allows Amex to assess what impact the complaint has had on longer-term customer behaviour. Based upon this, Amex can assess the effectiveness of its complaints-handling efforts and make new offers to customers who seem to be defecting. If customers indicate that they are likely to close their account, a separate call will be made to make offers such as waiving the annual management charge to encourage the customer to continue using the card.

4. Service-quality goals

Customer and employee satisfaction surveys help businesses set service-quality goals so that employees have targets to aim for. Many companies link employee bonuses to the attainment of customer satisfaction levels as this helps highlight the importance of customer service. Here are some examples of organizations that set goals around complaint handling.

A key measure of success at hotel chain Hilton is the number of complaints resolved within the unit. Only 2 per cent of complaints are escalated to the business's central complaints unit. Property managers suffer financially if a complaint is escalated to the central unit. Not only will they pay the cost of resolution, they also receive a fine, which for a Diamond customer is $200. Guest Assistance pass details of the complaint to the hotel, which has 48 hours to resolve with the customer and report back. Guest Assistance then calls the customer to ensure he or she is satisfied. If not, Guest Assistance can offer up to two nights' free accommodation in any hotel, the cost of which is passed back to the hotel where the complaint originated.

First direct is striving to better understand the business case for improving its complaints-handling process and is assessing the financial and longer-term benefits of the effort and investment. The bank undertook a project to introduce more sophisticated tools to estimate the costs and value of dealing effectively with complaints, and is trying to formulate a measure of 'customer experience' that will help it to determine the lifetime value of a customer.

To arrive at a lifetime value for the customer, first direct has to estimate how much the customer experience is enhanced or degraded, depending upon how well or badly a complaint is handled. It is anticipated that this will also help it to predict longer-term customer satisfaction, profitability and loyalty.

Hotel group Hilton is able to quantify the impact on the bottom line for each individual hotel of excellent versus poor service recovery efforts, and explain the business case that stops customers 'falling out the hole in the bottom of the bucket that managers need to fill through extra sales and marketing efforts'.

5. Customer-driven processes

Another method of creating a customer focus is to look at the processes your organization adopts from a customer's perspective. How easy is your company to do business with? Examples of businesses focusing on process improvement in terms of complaints include GE. It is committed to continuous learning and improvement. To help call centre agents solve customer problems more effectively and efficiently, it has invested $10 million in developing its Answer Centre. This large database holds answers to over 750,000 possible customer questions, so that when a customer calls with a problem the agent can enter a key word or phrase to bring the necessary information up. As new problems arise, they are researched and added to the database with key findings highlighted.

Finally, to reduce complaints, airline Cathay Pacific aims to head them off in advance by changing the service delivery process to reflect what it knows the customer wants. This is evidenced by rapid monitoring and action by head office (daily review event reports and a decision as to whether to contact customers before they have a chance to call the airline) and customization of initiatives.

When a customer experience has been poor, it tries to recapture loyalty by making sure the next trip is better. It finds out when the customer next plans to travel and offers an upgrade to a higher class of travel. It makes certain the service manager on the next flight seeks out the customer and speaks face to face (which Cathay believes is more personal). In management's view, customer emotions cannot be standardized, and therefore Cathay's response cannot be standardized.

Cathay has focused on both staff and line management by doing the following:

- persuading management to trust the judgement of their staff;
- providing access to customer information (history and value) to customer-facing staff;
- training staff on how to make decisions and use their judgement – when to say 'yes' and when to say 'no', based on a combination of customer value/class of travel/nature of complaint, and training staff to say 'no' politely, especially around policy complaints.

6. People development and empowerment

Best-practice customer-service organizations provide training and development in customer-service skills, attitudes and behaviours. They coach and develop their service leaders as well as their team members. They ensure that people are trained and empowered to resolve complaints as quickly and efficiently as possible.

Some examples of how this relates to complaint management are:

Taj Group ensures that it has created a culture based upon integrity, understanding, excellence, unity and responsibility. There is a clear model for business excellence and improvement that provides a framework within which to set targets and monitor performance. Their philosophy is that every complaint is justified.

Confidence is placed in that first point of contact to deal effectively with the situation. However, the customer also expects that, if so desired, he or she can be referred to management.

The philosophy of frontline staff is, 'Whatever is in my power, I will do; and if it's not within my power, I'll find someone else who can do it' (advocacy).

If a complaint recorded on the system is not resolved within set timeframes, it is automatically escalated to the Front Office Manager and then to the General Manager if necessary.

A complaint is closed only when it is confirmed that the problem has been fixed and the customer's satisfaction has been confirmed, the customer has received an apology and the problem has been referred to the area of function that will ensure it is not repeated. Representatives from each function meet weekly to analyse complaints data. They are responsible for root-cause analysis.

While Taj Group advocates resolution at the front line closest to the customer, there is a Customer Relations Team. All customer-relations staff have the same discretion as the Vice President of Customer Relations to offer refunds, etc. Management gives Customer Relations four simple instructions:

- Take time to listen.
- Use your good judgement.
- Apply commercial sense.
- Make the customer happy.

Management believe that if staff understand the full picture of business and are given sufficient training and development and freedom (empowerment), they will make the right decisions.

Staff at first direct are encouraged to take the initiative to resolve customer complaints and to look for solutions. Importantly they know that they will not be punished for going outside their job description. If it is felt that the staff did exceed their limits, first direct would look for learning points afterwards and coach out the mistakes, but not apply any sanction or discipline. Staff are also expected to contribute suggestions for improvement as part of their overall role.

At Enterprise Rent-A-Car, branch managers have been trained to look customers in the eye and tell them, 'I am really sorry. That is not the way we want this to be. What can I do to make it right?' The basic rule is always to fix the problem at the branch – do not let a dissatisfied customer walk out the door because you will never see them again.

If anyone is less than satisfied after resolution as part of the follow-up survey, they are asked if it is OK for the branch manager to contact them within 24 hours. Such an outcome is viewed as the branch manager having failed in his or her duty.

7. Communication, reward and recognition

Successful service organizations talk to customers at every opportunity. They put customer service on all their meeting agendas. They recognize and reward individuals who go out of their way to provide excellent service.

Global hotel chain Ritz Carlton has daily 'line-ups' so that all 22,000 staff have a meeting with their supervisor, manager, the vice president or chief executive of their location at the start of their shift. No more than 15 minutes is spent on this two-way communication, but it covers all the essential items, from which VIPs are staying in the hotel today to staff suggestions. What is particularly impressive and sets Ritz Carlton apart is that everyone across the world discusses the same subject every day – one of the 20 basics taken in turn.

Some of these basics include:

- It is the responsibility of each staff member to create a work environment of teamwork and (seamless) lateral service so that the needs of our guests and each other are met every day.
- Each staff member is empowered (up to $2,000 per incident).
  For example, when a guest has a special need or has a problem, you should break away from your normal duties and resolve the issue.

8. Sustaining a customer focus

Best-practice companies do not see customer service as a one-off 'campaign' or 'initiative'. For them customer care is a way of life, it is part of the culture of the organization. These businesses continually measure and monitor customer satisfaction and benchmark themselves against the competition. They ensure that improvements are made in the levels of service that they give on an ongoing basis. After all, customer expectations are constantly increasing. What is best practice today will not be so in the future.

These firms recognize that feedback, whether positive or negative, helps the organization to improve.

Staff at first direct are encouraged to take the initiative to resolve customer complaints and to look for solutions. Importantly, they know that they will not be punished for going outside their job description. If it is felt that staff did exceed their limits, first direct would take the opportunity to look for learning points afterwards and coach out the mistakes, but not apply discipline or sanction.

Staff are expected to contribute suggestions for improvement as a part of their overall role. The company supports this process by setting aside time for staff to get together informally to discuss problems and issues that they are encountering, so that suggestions can be made on how to tackle them and manage them out.

Four Seasons' culture is based upon giving staff dignity, respect and confidence to do the right thing for the customer. Frontline staff are empowered to make good a customer's disappointment. The primary aim at Four Seasons is to rebuild the relationship immediately, with no need to escalate. The cost of an escalated complaint is passed back to the hotel. There is no limit on the amount of compensation a general manager of a hotel can give to a customer, and therefore there is little reason for a complaint ever to escalate beyond the hotel.

Managers create a 'no fear' culture to ensure complaints are recorded. If a complaint is received after the guest has left, the complaint is passed to the general manager in the hotel who then has 24 hours to respond. An early call (acknowledgement) from the general manager cuts in half the impact of the complaint even if it takes longer to investigate.

The group CEO reads and responds to all complaints and compliments he receives. He contacts staff to congratulate them when they have received a compliment and will respond to the guest once he has a report from the general manager of the hotel regarding the disposition of the customer's complaint. If it is a particularly severe complaint, the CEO will call the manager personally.

Summary

Look at the eight characteristics and identify what your organization can do to embed a culture of customer focus where complaints are viewed positively and welcomed for the learning they provide. Rather than being a lone voice in your organization, I recommend that you share the learning from this. In particular I recommend you either being a sponsor, or you finding a sponsor for improvements in the way you handle complaints in your business.

I hope that you have found this book a useful guide to best practice in complaint management and that it has inspired you to start or continue your journey to put the customer at the heart of your organization.

Sarah Cook
The Stairway Consultancy Ltd
www.thestairway.co.uk

APPENDIX
How customer-centric is your business?

Use this assessment to identify your organization's degree of customer-centricity

Look at the questions below and respond appropriately.

If you feel that your answer is absolutely *yes* – a rating of 5 should be shown in the appropriate box.

If you feel that your answer is absolutely *no* – a rating of 1 should be shown in the appropriate box.

If you feel that your answer lies somewhere between these extremes – that is, it is partial – write 2, 3 or 4, to reflect your view.

If you feel that you cannot answer the question – write a 0 to reflect a *don't know* answer.

If you feel that the question does not apply to your business or function, please enter *N/A* in the box.

A. Vision and values

Question	Your score
A1 Is there an absolute belief, from top to bottom, that business growth and profitability is dependent upon customer satisfaction, retention and loyalty?	_____
A2 Are the organization's values published in a clear, concise and meaningful way?	_____
A3 Were the organizational values, if in place, developed with input from colleagues at all levels?	_____
A4 Is the main thread of the organization's goals based on the objective of building a customer-focused business?	_____
A5 Do all employees have a clear vision of how customers should be treated?	_____
A6 Is the organization's marketing strategy based upon giving customers a value-added service that differentiates you from competitors?	_____
A7 Does customer service genuinely sit at the top of the agenda in your business?	_____
TOTAL SCORE	_____

B. Continual customer research

	Question	Your score
B1	Do we have a clear and well-defined picture of the present and potential customers that the organization is aiming to serve?	_____
B2	Does the organization regularly conduct research with customers to determine what services they need and want?	_____
B3	Do managers at all levels regularly speak to customers, seeking their opinions on our service levels?	_____
B4	Does the organization share customer research with employees at all levels?	_____
B5	Does the organization have an effective system in place for customers to feed back their comments and observations about service levels?	_____
B6	Does the organization use customer research to change systems, procedures and processes?	_____
B7	Does the organization base its products and services on the genuine requirements of customers?	_____
	TOTAL SCORE	_____

C. Customer-centric organization structure

Question	Your score
C1 Does the organizational structure enable you to give customers what they are asking for?	_____
C2 Does the organizational structure make it easy for your customers to understand and do business with you?	_____
C3 When the business designs or make changes to the organizational structure, does it consider the needs of customers?	_____
C4 Does the business regularly review the structure of the organization to improve service levels?	_____
C5 Does the organizational structure reflect the importance of the internal customer also?	_____
C6 Does everyone in the organization have measurable accountability for customer service?	_____
C7 Does the organization encourage people to recognize the needs of internal as well as external customers?	_____
TOTAL SCORE	_____

D. Service-delivery processes and practices

	Question	Your score
D1	Have your service-delivery processes been designed more for the convenience and satisfaction of your customers rather than your own convenience?	_____
D2	Are the forms and documents used in your service-delivery processes customer friendly?	_____
D3	In designing a service-delivery process, does the organization start by defining the end result for the customer, and then develop the parts of the system needed to bring about that result?	_____
D4	Are your service-delivery processes flexible and adaptable enough to meet the requirements of customers?	_____
D5	Are your internal service-delivery processes related to customer service simple, flexible, easy to understand and user friendly?	_____
D6	Does the organization compare its service-delivery processes to those of competitors and revise them accordingly to improve the service?	_____
D7	Does the organization revise its service processes to remove blockages that make it difficult for customers to do business with it?	_____
	TOTAL SCORE	_____

E. Service-leadership competencies

Question	Your score
E1 Do all managers demonstrate, by their own behaviour, their commitment to achieving the highest levels of customer satisfaction and quality?	_____
E2 Is the management style in your organization highly participative?	_____
E3 Is responsibility and authority pushed down to the lowest levels possible?	_____
E4 Do managers talk to their teams regularly about customer service?	_____
E5 Does the performance-management system emphasize the importance of customer-focused behaviours?	_____
E6 Does the performance-management system reward people who demonstrate customer-focused behaviours?	_____
E7 Do managers readily acknowledge service excellence providers?	_____
TOTAL SCORE	_____

F. Measurement of service efficiency and customer satisfaction

Question	Your score
F1 Does the organization have quantified measurements of service efficiency for all key customer-contact roles?	_____
F2 Does the organization have quantified measurements of service effectiveness in terms of customer satisfaction?	_____
F3 Does the organization tell employees at all levels the results of customer-satisfaction surveys?	_____
F4 Does the organization use customer surveys, either written, telephone or online, to measure service satisfaction?	_____
F5 Does it really view complaints as an opportunity to improve?	_____
F6 Does it make it easy for customers to complain?	_____
F7 If a customer-service compliment is received, do managers provide direct face-to-face feedback to the employee concerned?	_____
TOTAL SCORE	_____

G. Creating the service excellence environment

	Question	Your score
G1	Does the organization operate an effective reward and recognition process for employees who provide service excellence?	
G2	Does the organization provide a good environment in the workplace that encourages staff to provide service excellence to customers?	
G3	Do the organization's business premises reflect a commitment towards service excellence?	
G4	Is the telephone technology in the organization designed for customer and service-giver convenience, efficiency and superior service delivery?	
G5	Does the organization regularly look at the environment facing its customers and seek to identify improvements?	
G6	Do you have efficient and sufficient work equipment to provide an excellent service to customers?	
	TOTAL SCORE	

H. Training and development of service skills

	Question	Your score
H1	Do new employees receive guidance regarding service standards and commitment to excellence prior to starting work?	_____
H2	Do employees receive proper technical (that is, product, systems, equipment) training to ensure that they are equipped to service customers?	_____
H3	Do employees receive sufficient service-skills training?	_____
H4	Does the organization have service standards to which new employees are trained?	_____
H5	When the business changes a service process, does it adequately communicate this to and train employees?	_____
H6	Does the organization invest sufficiently in service skills training?	_____
H7	Does the organization provide effective routes for career progression?	_____
	TOTAL SCORE	_____

Score sheet

Calculate the average scores for each category. Transfer the scores to the areas below. Then compare the scores. Identify what you do well and where you can improve.

A. Vision and values

Average score for this category: ___

B. Continual customer research

Average score for this category: ___

C. Customer-centric organization structure

Average score for this category: ___

D. Service delivery processes and practices

Average score for this category: ___

E. Service leadership competencies

Average score for this category: ___

F. Measurement of service efficiency and customer satisfaction

Average score for this category: ___

G. Creating the service excellence environment

Average score for this category: ___

H. Training and development of service skills

Average score for this category: ___

Consider what action you can take to increase your organization's customer focus, who you need to engage in the process and how you will do this.

REFERENCES

Aspect Customer Service Trends (2011) [Online] **www.customerservicetrends.com**

Gallwey, T (1986) *The Inner Game of Tennis*, Pan

Global Call Centre Project Report [Online] **www.ilr.cornell.edu/ globalcallcenter/upload/GCC-Intl-Rept-UK-Version.pdf**

Global coaching survey (2006) *Fortune* Magazine, October

Institute of Customer Service Survey [Online] **www.instituteofcustomerservice.com/1844/ UK-Customer-Satisfaction-Index-results.html**

Rucci, A, Kim, S and Quinn, R (1998) The employee–customer profit chain at Sears, *Harvard Business Review*, January, pp 10–26

Spitzer, D (1995) *SuperMotivation*, ANACOM

Technical Assistance Research Program (TARP) Studies 1979–2010 [Online] **www.tarp.com**

Tripp, T and Gregoire, Y (2011) When unhappy customers strike back on the internet, *MIT Sloan Management Review*, Spring, **52** (3), pp 36–44

Whitmore, J (2009) *Coaching for Performance: GROWing Human Potential and Purpose – The principles and practice of coaching and leadership*, Nicholas Brearley

INDEX